The Geometry of Energy
How to Meditate

Ethan Indigo Smith

~**Dedicated to your individuation.**

4

Chapter list

Introduction

Points, Lines, Circles and Spheres

The Ethereal Breath

The Point

Their Points

The Lines

Cutting Cords

The Planes

Clearing Collective Consciousness

The Solid

Taking the Space

The Geometry of Mandala

Summation of Vibration

Description of Ascension

Unity Consciousness

Introduction

Geometry directly assists our understanding of the physical world. Meditation directly assists our understanding of our inner world. Sacred geometry enhances our comprehension of reality and sensitivity to subtle energy by combining meditation practices and spiritual teachings with geometric principles and ideas.

Sacred geometry enables our understanding of the outer world, of our inner world, and an assortment of unexpected subjects and objects. *The Geometry of Energy How to Meditate* unites sacred geometry principles with meditation practices toward enhanced understanding of meditation and increased comprehension of self, and of surroundings, and the unexpected. With such enhancements unfold unexpected potential.

Meditation and geometry are tools. The tools are valuable in and of themselves, but mostly in how they enable us, sometimes unexpectedly. When we are equipped with a higher understanding of a tool it becomes more and more profoundly useful. *The Geometry of Energy How to Meditate* provides comprehension of meditation tools through the four dimensions of sacred geometry toward profound enhancement.

Let none ignorant of geometry enter.

It's said this phrase was above the doorway to Plato's school of philosophy and metaphysics. Why is an understanding of geometry so important to gaining further knowledge of philosophy and metaphysics? To begin with, when one understands geometry, and specifically the four dimensions of geometry, one can conceptualize the subtleties of different spaces, vibrations, and dimensions. Such conceptual capability enhances fundamentally and creatively.

The sign on the door to metaphysics school illustrates that geometry is important to further understanding all the varying dynamics of physics and metaphysics. The four dimensions of geometry in particular are helpful because they open our ability to imagine and understand new dimensions of the physical world as well as the energetic worlds. Through the mathematical and meditative correspondences of the four dimensions with subtle vibrations, understanding geometry can open our ability to better understand and potentiate meditation, revealing new dimensions of the world and within ourselves.

Geometry focuses on enhancing our understanding of the external and tangible. Meditation focuses on enhancing our understanding of the internal and intangible. Unification of geometrical constructs and meditative concepts enhances our understanding of our surroundings and ourselves. The combination of geometry and meditation is sacred geometry in being rather than in art form.

The four dimensions of geometry reveal the four dimensions of meditation exemplifying the spiritual aspects of sacred geometry via the physical aspects. The Geometry of Energy enhances our potential the same way mastering applicability of tools enables transcendence of the scope of their original design.

Pythagoras is known as a great mathematician, philosopher and sacred geometer. He is among the first known teachers to combine mathematics and metaphysics into sacred geometry and is credited with many discoveries beyond spiritual ones. Pythagoras is credited with celebrating the following expression of utmost import, "Know thyself, and thou shalt know the Universe and God." The Egyptian metaphysics schools also put forth the same idea.

The four dimensions of sacred geometry provide a way to comprehend energy outside of ourselves, and more importantly, energy within ourselves through enhanced meditation comprehension. The four dimensions reveal a lucid meditation formula, common among innumerable practices, uniting mathematics and meditation in metaphysics, contributing to enhanced understanding of our self, of our true nature, and overall enhanced being.

Pythagoras and Plato and many great thinkers across time alluded to the deeper potential meanings of geometry beyond mathematics, into subjects sacred. Pythagoras also developed and expanded many geometrical constructs and concluded essentially that geometry and mathematics were derived from and led one to a an enhanced understanding of God, or godliness, or subtle energy. It is my belief that the reason there are these relationships between God and Geometry as Pythagoras alluded, and between meditation and mathematics, is largely because of the relationship of the four dimensions of geometry with meditation and subtle energy, resulting in The Geometry of Energy.

Metaphysics is about individuation. No matter the esoteric or exoteric instruction and origins the focus is self-development. All metaphysical schools Hermetic, Socratic, Freemasonic, or otherwise, and all religious studies included or rather specifically originally were oriented around, self-development, transcending the material. Whether one studies Hermetics or The Bible one is familiar with the term or idea, 'know thyself.' Knowing yourself is the core function of learning and engages higher potential. Sacred geometry provides a universal mathematical structure enabling understanding of meditation and conceptualization of energy toward better knowing self.

"If you know the enemy and know yourself, you need not fear the result of a hundred battles. If you know yourself, but not the enemy, for every victory gained you will also suffer a defeat. If you know neither the enemy nor yourself, you will succumb in every battle." ~Sun Tzu

"The knowledge of which geometry aims is the knowledge of the eternal." ~Plato

One of the most well-known symbols associated with freemasonry is a G in the middle of the compass and square. It is above the doorways or set as an emblem at Freemason halls today inferring the old motto, 'let none ignorant of geometry enter.'

The G is said to stand for many things including God or The Grand Architect of The Universe, geometry, generation, and gnosis - possibly the gnosis that accompanies fusing godly and earthly concepts and energies; or combining physical geometry and metaphysical meditation. The symbol represents contrasting energies coming together in the feminine compass and the masculine square in order to create.

The compass and square symbol is presented here to illustrate the continued recognition of the power of sacred geometry, and its relation to metaphysical schools, not to endorse Freemasonry, of course. It is presented here to relate that old metaphysical school slogan with the continued search for comprehension and understanding, not to endorse the secretive modern-day groups claiming to be offshoots of the same metaphysical schools.

The sacred geometry mediation pursuits are yours to practice and be. No earthly insignia can dictate you knowing yourself, your becoming. It is my hope and intention the sacred geometry lessons here will help you better comprehend the physical and metaphysical.

Points, Lines, Circles and Spheres

The Geometry of Energy is a meditation explores meditation and subtle energy through the four dimensions of geometry. In its simplicity and profundity is an empowering four step meditation process leading to individuation, as well as an enhanced understanding of meditation and subtle energy. The four dimensions of geometry lead to understanding of meditation and energies for psychological and spiritual cleansing our thinking and being. The process of meditation enables individuation, distinguished self-development. Through better understanding of meditation comes more refined benefits.

The Geometry of Energy utilizes the four dimensions of geometry to enable a higher understanding of meditation and energy through eclectic and esoteric lessons, and yet simple relationships, all geared towards refinement of self. The Geometry of Energy enhances understanding of meditative energies through mathematical constructs revealing the fundamentals in numerous specific meditation practices and spiritual teachings.

The four dimensions of geometry, the four ways to understand objects, and correspondingly subtle energies, are as points, lines, planes, and solids. Circles are the highest form of a plane, and spheres are the highest form of solid.

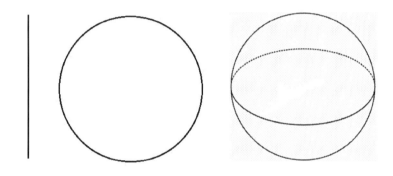

Points can represent anything, up to and including things the size of The Sun and things of no size at all. A point requires just one point to depict, obviously. A line requires a minimum of two points. A line can represent any distance, and implies little to no width, nor height. The third dimension is a plane. A plane can represent the space of a great field or of hardly any space at all, and implies there is little to no height. All planes require a minimum of three points, though infinite more points can be integrated for different shapes. The fourth dimension is a solid, a solid that might have no weight or be as great as The Sun. A solid requires a minimum of four points to depict making a four sided pyramid the simplest mathematical form, an infinite number of points can be integrated for differently shaped solids.

Geometrical rules relate to and address fundamentals of energy measurement. The idea of points without size, lines without width, shapes without height, and solids without weight address mathematical concepts and meditative energy constructs too.

Geometry means measurement of earth. The geometry of energy uses the four dimensions of measuring earth to measure earthen energies. The four dimensions of geometry have a magical quality to them, in that points may take up no space, lines may have no width, planes may have no height, and solids may have no weight. Energy forms in the same manner as the dimensions of geometry. Energy exists, but it may take up no space, have no width, no height, and no weight.

My experiences practicing different meditations and meditative movements led me to find corresponding dynamics in a wide range of practices that coincide with, and moreover directly reflect, the four dimensions of geometry. The shared dynamics are so powerful and related to so many diverse understandings, and so little had been written on the four dimensions of geometry relative to how much has been written of sacred geometry in total, that I had to meditate on and elaborate on the subject in this book. It soon became clear that the four dimensions of geometry were integral in meditation instruction and comprehension and also applicable to understanding subtle energy.

The Geometry of Energy explores meditation and subtle energy through mathematics, geometry, numerology and spiritual understandings. The Geometry of Energy provides meditation instruction, and offers a way to understand meditative energies toward individuation, toward your own personal development. The four types of energies related to the four dimensions of geometry result in a four step meditation process that potentiates your unique individuation, and yet is based on the universality of geometry.

Energy is vibration, in fact, everything is vibrational. The light we see and the sounds we hear are just energy vibrations coalesced differently. We ourselves are energy vibrations coalesced into conscious physical form and flow. Meditative energy vibrations can be a point up to and including a point that takes up no space, lines up to and including lines with no width, planes up to and including planes of no thickness, and solids up to and including volumes of no space, and the volume of entirety.

"Concerning matter, we have been all wrong. What we have called matter is energy, whose vibration has been so lowered as to be perceptible to the senses. There is no matter." ~Albert Einstein

The four dimensions of geometry relate to all things of substance, and subtle energies that appear to our senses to be without substance. Sunlight is energy vibration. Sunlight has been found to exist in the form of particles and waves. Particles are like energy points and waves are like energy lines. Abstractly there may be higher forms of light that may vibrate as planes and solids for we are certainly mostly incapable of awareness of all levels of reality. The less dense we are the lighter we become and the more sensitive to more obscure aspects and/or potentials of subtle energy.

I'm occasionally sensitive enough to at least postulate the subtle energies. Planes of light might correlate with sighted visions, being light vibrations we see or detect whether our eyes are open or closed. The solid forms of light are often noted as magical happenstance, that is to say the transmutation of solid into transparent, or transmutation of transparent into solidity.

"Infinities and indivisibles transcend our finite understanding, the former on account of their magnitude, the latter because of their smallness; Imagine what they are when combined." ~Galileo Galilei

There are an infinite assortment of points, lines, planes and solids. And yet points frequently take up no space. Lines are optimally straight making connection via shortest distance. Circles are the pinnacle plane shape containing the greatest area with the smallest length within the simplest and strongest form and flow. Spheres are the ultimate solid shape containing maximum volume by way of least surface area. Spheres like circles to planes are the simplest and strongest of solids.

Circles can be made up of an infinite number of lines and each line can be made up of an infinite number of points whereas spheres can be made up of an infinite number of faces or planes. The forms and flows of circles and spheres are similar. The geometrical energies of light in plane and solid form and flow, are mostly undetectable to our generally dense wake state/sleep state awareness. They are made up of infinite points, and of infinite planes, hence the visionary and magical aspects, for when reflections multiply infinitely, force multiples, and amazing and seemingly magical things occur.

Meditative energy comes in infinite variations, all of which can be broken down with the geometry of energy, into four types, points, lines, planes and solids representing concentration, connection, circulation and unity expansion. Each type is more infinitely reflective, and infinitely more magical with more potential.

The more you meditate the more sensitive you become to meditative energies and subtle energetic qualities. The more immersed in meditation the more release from the states of dulled consciousness takes place. The more immersed in meditation the more elevated the potential in one's observation and action. Meditation enhances comprehension of the basic and the esoteric like the higher forms of light energy, even the planes and solids, made up of coursing infinity. The Geometry of Energy enhances our comprehension of meditation.

In my own meditation experiences the many types of colorful subtle energies I sense in my frontal lobe or third eye, no matter their diversity, can all be understood in synchronicity with the constructs of the four dimensions of geometry. After further investigation into these concepts, it occurred to me the dimensions also provide powerful instruction for, and comprehension of meditation itself. Through the simple and sacred understandings demonstrated in the four dimensions of the geometry as revealed in numerous meditation teachings an intrinsic instruction on how to meditate reveals itself, as well as the construct to understand meditation and subtle energies.

The meditation instruction is based on the fourfold geometric dynamic, and enhanced through corresponding ancient and diverse meditation practices. In correspondence there is simplicity and potentiation. Corresponding information from diverse sources frequently represents a common denominator of truth. The most superfluous and most unnecessary parts fall away over time, whereas the most powerful aspects of any understanding, among any subject, remain steadfast and central.

Nearly all meditations and practices contain elements which correlate with the four dimensions of geometry, most overtly so, and some more subtly. Understanding the geometry of energy enhances comprehension of meditation itself beyond the particular practices explored, and subtle energy in total.

The Ethereal Breath

Energy flows with the flowing. Energy moves with movement. Chi or prana or electricity is not the blood or the breath, but moves within the flowing of each. The flowing of the breath makes it easier to attain and release more subtle energy. Developing the breath alone leads to highly rewarding experiences. Meditative breathing of all sorts can lead to profound experiences pertaining to development of health or capability. Developing breath control and moving energy through awareness can be an intoxicating or alternatively upsetting experience, but either way it's beneficial. It's simply a matter of moving through stagnancy and rigidity that can be upsetting or difficult.

The breath can heal all so to speak. Cancer for instance does not survive in an oxygenated environment. Healing physical trauma can be actualized through breath control. Potential force exhibited is also maximized through breath control. In my experience through developing my overall practice and intensity of certain sessions of practice, the breath moved and cleared so much energy I found I did not need a new breath as much as normally. The sensation is very much as if even though you've exhaled you're still full of oxygenated chi so urgency of the breath slows. Of all the elements the air offers the best access to energy through our breath.

Meditative breathing can be endlessly refined. The breath unifies the primal and ultimate profundity in its subtlety. No matter what changes in the world the importance of the breath is unchanged. No matter the modification or variation of meditation, the breath remains the most important, primal start to meditation and ultimate aspect of practically all meditations. The breath approaches the inner truth.

Understanding the breath is the simplest and most profound key to tapping into meditative energy. Perhaps the most essential thing to understand about the breath is every breath you ever take manifests in four distinct aspects; inhalation, pause full, exhalation, and pause empty.

In order to realize the breath, be mindful of the breath, note each aspect, and imagine each aspect lengthening and slowing. Imagine being with and being of the breath as you mindfully, consciously breathe. Elongate each part of the breath, deepen the breath. Breathe consciously and deeply, as if from your belly. Meditation is as complicated as breathing, it's something you have done your whole life, it merely requires shifting attention inward. Developing meditation is simply a matter of refinement of attention, and at the same time simplification of attention. And by going deeper inward, with the breath, we -somewhat counterintuitively- gain access to our inner world and understanding of the outer world more completely.

Breath is the basis of all life, the same as it is the basis of all meditation and meditative movement. Breath is the primary manner in which we all obtain life energy. The other three are as water, food and prana or chi. When we our invigorated with chi we can slow the breath and decrease the need for food and water.

There are four important aspects of meditative breathing. It is important to breathe slowly, deeply, steadily, and consciously. It's commonly understood that most people do not breathe properly. Most people breathe from high points, like their shoulders. A complete yogi breath is a cyclical movement beginning from the lower belly moving upwards like a wave. There are numerous understandings of breath, and yet the main important factor is to breathe consciously.

There are many different forms of breathing, but balanced breathing is utilized most frequently. Balanced breathing means the four parts to one breath cycle are about equalized. The inhalations and exhalations are the same length of time to each other and the pause full and pause empty are the same length of time to each other too. For example 8 seconds in, 2 second pause, 8 seconds out, 2 second pause is a balanced breath cycle. Another balanced breath that can be more intense holds each aspect the same length, like a 10 second inhale, 10 second pause full, 10 second exhale, and 10 second pause empty.

There are four aspects of the breath and four forms of breath reflective of the Yin Yang theory as well. The four variations of breath in Yin Yang theory have to do with enhancing or elongating a pause in the breath cycle. Inhalations are Yang and contracting, and exhalations are Yin and releasing.

In order to stimulate building energy, accentuate the pause after inhalation. In order to stimulate releasing energy, accentuate the pause after the exhalation. These are the main two aspects like the main swirls in the Yin Yang.

In order to stimulate movement of building energy pause during the inhalation, then continue the rest of inhalation. And in order to stimulate the movement of releasing energy pause during exhalation, and then continue the rest of it.

Pausing the breath is recommended only after you have experience sitting in relaxed balanced breathing, and some may only want to practice balanced breath, the understanding of the concept is important even if not practicing.

Meditation practitioners from long ago would count the breath not in seconds, but heartbeats. Counting our heart beats and elongating the breath is enough alone to meditate on and helps us be more focused on our life center, fostering conditions to heighten our awareness and calm any mental chatter that prevents going more inward and becoming more mindful of subtleties.

There are innumerable variations of meditative breath, however in most all meditations awareness of the breath is a primarily important perception. Some more developed meditation practitioners move beyond focus on the breath, however even masters always come back to and mostly begin with the breath. For all of us focusing on the breath can calm the distracted monkey mind that swings from vine to vine, from thought to distracting thought. Trouble in meditation equates to, in general having a full mind, perceiving the breath allows us to be alternatively mindful on something constant and less erratic than other thoughts that usually fill our heads so as to begin and develop meditation.

Balanced breath is beneficial to balancing our energy, often all we need to recuperate and rejuvenate. Tai chi practice recommends breathing so slowly that if there were a feather at your nose it would not be moved. In order to be relaxed and thereby have energy run through you easier, only breathe to about 70% of lung capacity, and make sure to exhale entirely. One trick to check your breath posture is to stand up and inhale fully. If you have to reach your shoulders back to do so, your posture is not straight and you are using your shoulders to breathe, and not your belly.

Meditation is as simple as conscious breathing. Meditation is as simple as paying attention to two plus two, it's as simple as you becoming you. Being ourselves is easy, but reanimating our self in our true nature, after a lifetime of adhered collective constructs, mediations and social pressures layered onto our being, can be quite difficult. What can often be a transformation resembling that of a butterfly from cocoon to flight can also become like breaking layers of concrete as one rips apart one's shells as if opening up from the inside out.

The process is also a lot like a story of Hanuman the Hindu Monkey deity. Hanuman is depicted ripping his chest open to reveal his heart, his inner truth and to be open to energy. Meditation clears and cleans our psychology and spirituality so we are open to being in our authenticity. Social constructs of mediation layers shells of fakeness onto us, shells that we break through with meditation.

"The foundation of all mental illness is the unwillingness to experience legitimate suffering." ~Carl Jung

Meditation is therefore a process, and properly referred to as a practice, because sometimes the constructed obstructions that shell our true selves are thick and embedded deeply into our thinking and being. Sometimes there are knotty layers that slow the process of becoming our true nature and make it difficult. It is easy to be you. The difficulty may be in breaking through. Often enough beginning meditation is thusly the most difficult time because of the initial painful shifts, the cracking of our shells, and often enough after experiencing a bit of breaking many people turn around do not go through.

Meditation assists us to find our true nature and also become more powerful and positive. Meditation is the most powerful activity people are capable of. It is a tool to find our true nature and our true power, it is individuation practice. Meditation can be enhanced by refining our comprehension of it as well as refining its practice. The geometry of energy uses mathematics and geometry, to define meditation and expand its understanding.

Meditation has no theological or spiritual prerequisites, though the more you meditate the more spiritually curious and spiritually conscious you will likely become. Mathematics can be utilized to expand our comprehension of meditation and ultimately open the door to spirituality, as can spiritualty and theology but there is not a requirement to meditate. In fact any excuse not to meditate in itself is prerequisite of the capability or even necessity to meditate. If you think you are too busy, you are ready. If you are too hurt, it is the perfect opportunity, you are ready. And if you have never done it before, you are ready. Take every distraction, hindrance and difficulty as opportunity to meditate on higher vibration by ascending past the difficulty. This is the main beginning symbolism of the lotus flower. The lotus flower is impeccably beautiful and it only blooms in the muddy swamps.

"Sit in meditation twenty minutes a day, if you are too busy then you should sit one hour." ~Zen Saying

"These, as we find, are slow, yet sure, if there will be kept, not only the corrections made occasionally, once a month or such, might be the more often but the meditation; and in the meditation, don't meditate upon, but listen to the voice within. For prayer is supplication for direction, for understanding. Meditation is listening to the Divine within." ~Edgar Cayce

"It [meditation] is not musing, not daydreaming; but as ye find you bodies made up of the physical, mental and spiritual, it is the attuning of the mental body and the physical body to its spiritual source."
~Edgar Cayce

Meditation is a way to clean our psychology of negative burdensome and constricting densities to enhance our spiritual nature into more expansive and yet connected light being. It is true that even atheists can benefit from meditation, and true that they might not benefit as much, for being open to energy means being open to ideas and states of being, and being closed off to the idea of god closes you off from quite a bit of energy to say the least. With that in mind, the more open, loving and most importantly and sometimes most difficult, the more forgiving and accepting you are, the higher quality energy you can understand and assimilate.

A spiritual connection is developed during meditation no matter the mind, and I would dare say that lacking spirituality ardently and meditating ultimately would not gently mix. On the other hand many religious people do not believe in meditation and do not seem the least bit spiritual either. Spirituality and mediation mix well, but religious ardency, as well as atheist ardency, may not mix with meditation at all.

If you are religious, but not spiritual, or neither religious nor spiritual, you can still benefit from meditation and I suspect spiritual connection would develop despite you, though cracking through the mediation we all endure might be more uncomfortable that way. If you do not yet believe in the intangible spiritual nature of entirety, and merely believe in the power of our thinking and being when connected, just practice concentration, and imagine absorption of your individual self with a universal, evolved consciousness.

In Vedic and Buddhist practices there are considered to be three stages of higher meditation. There is Dharana; concentration or fixing the attention of mind onto one object or place. There is Dhyana; sustained concentration, whereby the attention continues to hold the same object despite fluctuations. And then there is Samadhi; deep absorption as opposed to deep concentration. Within these there are different phases too.

Meditation clears our inner house and such housecleaning can be, not so abstractly, related to certain teachings or suggestions in biblical scripture. The esoteric elaboration of Jesus Christ clearing his father's house relates in subtle, but profound ways. Jesus Christ clears his father's house of mediation from business, government and religion. Jesus cleans the psychological constructs of the meditative zones; the outer court, the holy place and the holy of holies.

15 On reaching Jerusalem, Jesus entered the temple courts and began driving out those who were buying and selling there. He overturned the tables of the money changers and the benches of those selling doves, 16 and would not allow anyone to carry merchandise through the temple courts. 17 And as he taught them, he said, "Is it not written: My house will be called a house of prayer for all nations?' But you have made it a den of robbers. ~Mark 11:15 – 11:17

Spiritual teachings contain literal and metaphorical lessons, and often more layers. Ancient temples across the world were designed in this manner, where the architectural temple symbolized our own temples, ourselves, our own bodies. Sometimes the temples symbolized our entire body and sometimes parts of our bodies, like our brain. This resulted in the correlation of temple of worship with temple of our heads. In Biblical text there is known to be three aspects of the temple, the outer court, inner court, and the holy of holies. Generally speaking the outer court corresponds with our body, the inner court for our mind, and the holy of holies for our higher spirit. In order to cleanse ourselves, our temples, meditation and meditative movement are utilized.

There are four physical forms of meditation posture; walking, standing, sitting and lying positions. Practice and refine them all. Adjust your practice to suit your tastes and change it so as to occasionally go outside your comfort zone. It is important to practice familiar concepts and also occasionally to do something new, and different. Sometimes a slight modification in meditation or activity can crack open shells that prevent you from being you. Sometimes we have to throw out old constructs that took hold, just like Jesus did. Variations of meditative movements assist you in your pursuit toward individuation, toward being your true nature as well as variation of experiences and learning.

The first phase of Dhyana of meditation is investigation, analysis, bliss one-pointedness. The second phase is joy, bliss one-pointedness and internal clarity where pure light is emitted. The third phase is bliss, one-pointedness, mindfulness, stabilization and insight. The fourth is completely pure equanimity, compassion for all, mindfulness, and neither pleasure nor pain. The text called The Noble Search relates four stages of Dhyana. The dynamic is presented with four forms of Dhyana and four phases of formless Dhyana.

First Dhyana

"Suppose that a wild deer is living in a wilderness glen. Carefree it walks, carefree it stands, carefree it sits, carefree it lies down. Why is that? Because it has gone beyond the hunter's range. In the same way, a monk — quite withdrawn from sensual pleasures, withdrawn from unskillful qualities — enters & remains in the first dhyana: rapture &

pleasure born from withdrawal, accompanied by directed thought & evaluation. This monk is said to have blinded Mara. Trackless, he has destroyed Mara's (Mara is a Buddhist trickster, and devil if you will) vision and has become invisible to the Evil One."

Second Dhyana

"Then again the monk, with the stilling of directed thoughts & evaluations, enters & remains in the second dhyana: rapture & pleasure born of composure, unification of awareness free from directed thought & evaluation — internal assurance. This monk is said to have blinded Mara. Trackless, he has destroyed Mara's vision and has become invisible to the Evil One."

Third Dhyana

"Then again the monk, with the fading of rapture, he remains equanimous, mindful, & alert, and senses pleasure with the body. He enters & remains in the third dhyana, of which the Noble Ones declare, 'Equanimous & mindful, he has a pleasant abiding.' This monk is said to have blinded Mara. Trackless, he has destroyed Mara's vision and has become invisible to the Evil One."

Fourth Dhyana

"Then again the monk, with the abandoning of pleasure & stress — as with the earlier disappearance of elation & distress — enters & remains in the fourth dhyana: purity of equanimity & mindfulness, neither-pleasure-nor-pain. This monk is said to have blinded Mara. Trackless, he has destroyed Mara's vision and has become invisible to the Evil One."

The infinitude of space (first formless Dhyana)

"Then again the monk, with the complete transcending of perceptions of [physical] form, with the disappearance of perceptions of resistance, and not heeding perceptions of diversity, [perceiving,] 'Infinite space,' enters & remains in the dimension of the infinitude of space. This monk is said to have blinded Mara. Trackless, he has destroyed Mara's vision and has become invisible to the Evil One."

The infinitude of consciousness

"Then again the monk, with the complete transcending of the dimension of the infinitude of space, [perceiving,] 'Infinite consciousness,' enters & remains in the dimension of the infinitude of consciousness. This monk is said to have blinded Mara. Trackless, he has destroyed Mara's vision and has become invisible to the Evil One."

The dimension of nothingness

"Then again the monk, with the complete transcending of the dimension of the infinitude of consciousness, [perceiving,] 'There is nothing,' enters & remains in the dimension of nothingness. This monk is said to have blinded Mara. Trackless, he has destroyed Mara's vision and has become invisible to the Evil One."

The dimension of neither perception nor non-perception

"Then again the monk, with the complete transcending of the dimension of nothingness, enters & remains in the dimension of neither perception nor non-perception. This monk is said to have blinded Mara. Trackless, he has destroyed Mara's vision and has become invisible to the Evil One."

The cessation of perception and feeling

"Then again the monk, with the complete transcending of the dimension of neither perception nor non-perception, enters & remains in the cessation of perception & feeling. And, having seen that with discernment, his mental fermentations are completely ended. This monk is said to have blinded Mara. Trackless, he has destroyed Mara's vision and has become invisible to the Evil One. Having crossed over, he is unattached in the world. Carefree he walks, carefree he stands, carefree he sits, carefree he lies down. Why is that? Because he has gone beyond the Evil One's range." ~From The Buddhist text The Noble Search.

    The ultimate goal of these considerations or phases is the cessation of perception and feeling, of ardency, and of mental clutter. These stages and understandings loosen the grips of our biological impulses, our need for stimuli, and our political/social mediation to unconsciously re-act out our basic and dense programming in the unfolding drama. When we lose our wild perceptions and feelings we encounter our true nature unburdened, and are able to refine ourselves and our connection inwardly and with our surroundings.

    Many religious institutions refuse to accept that meditation and meditative movement could assist individuals to encounter their true nature, or godliness. Of course many religions essentially force dogmatic ardency on others, insisting their way is the only way. In this manner alone individuation is completely counter to their constructs requiring followers. Meditation originates more in mathematics and timeless spiritual constructs rather than timely institutional framework.

"Science without religion is lame, religion without science is blind."
~Albert Einstein

There is so much to discover about that which we cannot quantify, the intangible, including energy that takes up no space. Mathematics and meditation are comprised of the intangible, but we can still experience both, and utilize both. Our dreams too are composed of nothing and yet real, just as our spiritual and psychological aspects are unquantifiable, and yet we could speak volumes on them.

The Geometry of Energy meditation instruction is based on building the power of individuation and built toward understanding unquantifiable energy. The Geometry of Energy can assist you toward expanding your individuation. Meditation leads to individuation. There are many ways to meditate, many formulas to expand the mind, some of the most simple are the most effective and some of them are profoundly related to mathematics and the four dimensions of geometry. Some of the most spiritual concepts are numerical and geometrical.

There are 3 numbers in the modern numerical system that generally are the same when seen directly, and when viewed as a mirror image. They are 1, 0, and 8. 108 is the most divine number in all numerology in all of history. The significance of 108, numerically and spiritually, cannot be overlooked. For a complete elaboration on 108 please read 108 Steps to Be in The Zone.

108 is the most sacred number among Tibetan, Indian, Chinese and most Asian cultures. 108 can be used as the simplest meditation instruction there is, all on its own. Interestingly enough, and as further validity of The Geometry of Energy and further exemplification of the beauty of 108, when the four dimensions of geometry are depicted next to each other as point, line, circle and sphere they very much look like 108 or rather .108 to be specific.

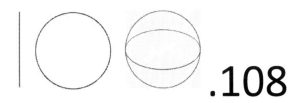

Many meditations, no matter how esoteric and dynamic, begin with the 108 construct, though not necessarily explicitly so. Be 1 with the breath, allow 0 things to coalesce from the past, positive or negative, in order to then tap into the infinite within, the infinite of entirety, or anything of the infinite, symbolized of course by 8. Use 108 to settle into a meditative mind state, to remind you how to comprehensively become meditative, to unite with the breath. 108 also represents and unites the breath. In yoga traditions it's said people take 10800 breaths every 12 hours, 10800 breaths every day and every night.

If the 108 idea does not suit you, just be one with the breath in order to settle into a meditative state. Take note of the breath and be present with each aspect of the breath fully. Focus your thoughts on inhalations and exhalations as they occur. The most important aspect of beginning meditation, and the matter that remains of pinnacle importance, is the breath. The breath itself can provide the mechanical operation of magical function. The breath is our key, as coalesced consciousness, to develop and connect with our true nature and experience intangible subtleties.

There are so many ways to breathe, but the most important thing is breathe consciously and to concentrate, but not too hard, on breathing from as deeply down as possible. Most people are indeed so stuck in their heads that they do not breathe deeply, in fact they breathe using their shoulders. While breathing from deep down consciously note the four aspects of breath; the inhale, the exhale and the pauses, whether accentuated or minimalized.

Be one with the breath by simply paying attention to each aspect of breath. Many variations exist to develop individuation, and meditation on the breath in the present is one of them, if not the ultimate direction of such meditation. To gain a meditative state slow down the breath, and focus on the breath, this simple act allows access to higher levels of consciousness, of calm within and understanding of intangibles out. One simple method to be one with the breath is to count the breaths, counting every cycle as one breath. See how many full breaths you can count without being distracted.

There are four parts of one breath and there are four main aspects of consciousness as reflected by the revered and ancient symbol, Aum. The first two stages are experienced by practically everyone on a daily basis; the sleep state and wake state are the bottom portions of the symbol. The second two are deep sleep state and deep awakening state, deep awakening or the transcendental state is on the upper right, the point beyond the curved line, also known as the point behind the veil.

We are all capable of deep thinking and being, instead of the dense waking and dreaming we mostly tend to go through on a day to day basis. After being thoroughly indoctrinated to think and be a certain way by societal constructs most people enter the third and fourth states infrequently, if ever. As we meditate, we clear the obstructions set upon us during influential traumatic experiences and simple socialization. We return to our true nature, expanding consciousness and enlightenment as opposed to the denseness and dimness we most frequently are under and impose.

The instruction of the Geometry of Energy is a process for becoming. It could be extrapolated and demonstrated in one particular way that could be decent for all. However by leaving it open, by using the four dimensions of geometry as a foundation and in examination, the mathematical process can be refined in unique ways. As a tool it can work best for everyone, as we all use the same mathematics as suitable. The main construct of the meditation instruction born out of the four dimensions of geometry is that it does not have any ardency, or rigidity, there is no mandatory time or process constraint. The design of your meditation is left entirely up to you. The book presents comprehension through the structure in the geometry of energy allowing for individual development in your own form and flow. The development of your own process is as much a practice of refinement toward individuation and empowerment as meditation itself. The Geometry of Energy expands meditation comprehension rather than presenting a single specific meditation instruction.

If the thought of designing your own meditation is too much to think about right now, trust it will happen and know that simple directions from many practices are presented anyhow. With the geometry of energy, your meditation is part of your personal individuation and yet in correlation with many outstanding mathematic understandings, refined meditation processes, and numerous spiritual practices.

There are so many modifications and variations of so many styles and forms of tai chi chuan because it is an art of individuation. The instrument, that is the form, adjusts to the individual's flow. The form and flow is individualized, and if it were done ardently similar it would not be relaxed, and not yield the same results. Everything energetic, artistic and athletic illustrates the power of individualization and individuation, including of course, meditation. Individuation leads to unique style and grace when you're doing the same thing that many others might do too.

"…'Spirit' comes from the Latin word "to breathe." What we breathe is air, which is certainly matter, however thin. Despite usage to the contrary, there is no necessary implication in the word "spiritual" that we are talking of anything other than matter (including the matter of which the brain is made), or anything outside the realm of science. On occasion, I will feel free to use the word. Science is not only compatible with spirituality; it is a profound source of spirituality. When we recognize our place in an immensity of light years and in the passage of ages, when we grasp the intricacy, beauty and subtlety of life, then that soaring feeling, that sense of elation and humility combined, is surely spiritual." ~Carl Sagan

In many ways when we breathe in meditation, we do very much activate our respiratory system, our re-spirit-atory system. Through the breath we can most easily re-spirit, reinvigorate and reintegrate the ethereal and subtle energies of the universal with the individual. The specific practice involved and the meditative movement integrated with the breath matters less than the simple mindfulness of your breath.

The point represents concentration, the line represents connection, the plane represents circulation, and the solid represents unity expansion.

The Point

"Where there is matter, there is geometry." ~Johannes Kepler

The four dimensions meditation begins with focusing on a clear point. Focusing on a point, and perhaps most particularly on your center point of being, your essential and divine spark, can bring about tremendous clarity quickly, enabling further deepening of meditative states. The point represents concentration, a focused clarity.

When we first set self into a meditative positioning our minds might sometimes be racing a thousand different places, chewing on a thousand different thoughts, running around a thousand different fantasies, basking in emotions, playing in plans, and juggling dozens of abstracts, all at once, but when we focus on the point all those swirl away or into the point, and we regain our higher focus and mental clarity. The point represents presence, our being present, our concentration. Begin by focusing on a point of energy, your point of clarity and divinity in concentrate.

The four dimensions of geometry are related to matter, of course, and energy, and also are related to time. The point of course represents the present, the singularity of now. The line represents the past and its nothingness yet connection, and the plane can represent the future and its unfolding potential. And that is present, past and future, whereas the solid being everything, represents timelessness, the everything, the entirety beyond measure, time beyond time, the Akashic space. Akasha means ethereal space, suggesting an all permeating volume. Focus on a point of concentration to be in the present.

This construct is of course similar to 108 being reflective of present, past, future. The unsaid fourth aspect is timelessness, or the Akashic Field, or rather the volume of entirety from where intuition originates. 1 is for the present point, 0 for the past, 8 for the future and the unsaid is the Akashic volume of timelessness. Geometrically speaking, the difference between a plane and a field is a plane has no height, and a field does. The Akashic Field is essentially the intangible wave of universal consciousness which permeates everywhere, and yet is immeasurable, here and beyond, everywhere and nowhere, the void.

Just as there are four ways to geometrically understand objects and energy, there are four ways to understand time, as the present, past, future, and timelessness. Recognition of these four aspects of time enhances the ability to sense subtle energies of timelessness. If this is too abstract for you right now, don't worry it really doesn't matter relative to the overall meditation instruction and perhaps the meditation itself will provide correlation and understanding.

"All moments, past, present and future, always have existed, always will exist." ~Kurt Vonnegut

"The distinction between the past, present and future is only a stubbornly persistent illusion." ~Albert Einstein

    The more we don't obsess over time, over how long we meditate and how long it takes, the more we can focus on how we experience meditation. The less we focus on time, the more constructive we can be. The less we consider the time meditation takes, the more time meditation makes. You might need to sleep less and might require less time to do your work with a clear mind for instance.

    As you settle into a meditative mind state, being one with the breath, clearing past densities, allowing zero past experiences to coalesce so as to be more open to the infinite, it is important to focus, generate and stir your potentiated energy toward individuation. The geometry of energy meditation is a helpful idea for this process.

    The meditation presented and the format provided give busy minded people who believe they think too much to meditate, and those who believe they would love to meditate but don't know how, a refined course of inward action. Some meditations may be better than others, but mainly there are just more dedicated practitioners who reap more rewards. All meditations make returning to our true nature easier, which in itself may not be easy. All meditations can increase our mental, physical and spiritual capacities. Meditation is relaxing and invigorating, but in order to turn off the chatter within to begin we often need to turn on thinking about in a direction with intention and attention.

"Where there is matter there is geometry." ~Johannes Kepler

Everything begins as a point. The widely celebrated symbol of the flower of life begins as a seed, with symbols within it such as the tree of life, then it flowers from a planar depiction into the three dimensional form and flow, the solid. Some have proposed a four stage process of plant growth, germination of the seed, pre-flowering growth upward toward the Sun, pollination and seed dispersal into the volume.

'Being on point' is the seed for attuned awareness during any number of earthly practices including meditation processes. In geometry there are four dimensions of understanding, four ways to understand tangible objects, and in meditation there are four ways to understand intangible energies. The first energetic potentiation is to focus on being in your center, and on eventually being in your heart center, a single point that brings esoteric meaning to the expression 'the heart of the matter.' Imagine the power and light that just a speck of the sun has, and imagine this power in the point inside of you blooming warmth and light throughout your clarity and your true nature.

We are made up of coalesced light energy. Points of energy are manifest as chakras within us, whereas lines are the meridians also called nadis in yoga traditions (astral energy tubes) which connect the chakras and the energy flow. The planes are the linear consciousness we emit and detect, and solids equate to our auras or the love imbued in us, and surrounding us.

Begin to focus on exploring the point of light and being the point of light within you and your otherwise clear hollowness. Imagine it fill your clarity up like heat in a balloon. Or if it suits you imagine yourself as being a point of light entirely. You can experiment with where this point is. You may direct it to an injury and or position it to be in the mental, guttural or in the heart center essentially.

Ultimately we are practicing to return to our true selves, in the heart center. Mostly we have been taken away from our true center, to our heads or to our guts. We are steered into states of mental and physical craving, always in need of entertainment and edibles without care. So in meditation, eventually, after exploring the position and situation of the point try to bring it to your heart center.

Most people exist in a state of consciousness where their primal guttural center connects with ego mental center to control their thinking and being. Some might be more in their gut, and others more in their logical heads, but the heart is bypassed and minimalized. The lack of care and lack of being in our heart center with internal clarity is visible in how people relate to the outside world, how we collectively clutter and litter and pollute. Being in our heart and leading through our heart center is our true nature, our true unadulterated nature, unhindered by collective societal influences and traumatization.

"The heart and the mind has the shortest distance but has the longest journey." ~TS Eliot

One of the most profound and powerful meditation practices uses this point of concentration in its order of operations as a beginning. Naropa yoga is one of the most esoteric and possibly one of the most transformative yogas practiced and shared today. The six yogas of Naropa are rooted in Indian and Tibetan practices. The first yoga is that of Tummo, the practice of developing inner fire. The main aspect of this practice is imagining a single point of flame inhabiting and enlightening the entire hollow physical form and flow. Tummo practice begins each of the following of the Six Yogas too, making it intrinsic to the entirety. Many other meditations practice initial focus on being and opening the point in the heart center as well, Tummo of Naropa is among the oldest, most profound and most powerful. It focuses on the clarity of body and the idea that one tiny point of heat/light/love, that divine spark, fills the energy body with this psychic heat of Tummo. The P'howa Yoga, the final yoga of Naropa Yoga involves the direct transference of consciousness, as a single point.

Indian and Tibetan meditation methods include considering the point aspect as a point of light, sometimes related to a drop, and a seed. The point is called bindu in India and tigle in Tibet. In fact these traditions, along with many other metaphysical ideas, suggest that we are eternal, that we are points of light before our birth and coalesce into seven density light beings if you will. When we are in touch with our essence, our point of light, or point of light consciousness, we are more in balance and more in control. When we are balanced and in control we can accelerate our ascension and our comprehension/progression concerning anything we choose. One can meditate on being in each chakra as your point and embodying the character of each chakra as you proceed, from the top chakra downwards and the bottom chakra back upward.

Another simple meditation process that utilizes the point construct is known as the heart center meditation. Imagine going inward into your heart consciousness, where your heart's consciousness resides. It's as if you go into a room, your heart, and then to a throne, the point where your heart's consciousness resides. Be singularly focused on the point and allow everything else to sway passed, as it comes up acknowledge it and let it go by.

Stay here focused on this spiritual self-centeredness of the point for a time. Imagine a time during your life, during your day or during your recent story in which you were focused and on point. In your meditation imagine being like a point in nature, like a raindrop, or like a seed.

Seeds grow despite conditions set up against them. They grow into plants that take the space from stones which prior had so imposed difficulty for the seeds to take root. Despite the stones, despite appearances and despite figuratively what everyone says the seed bursts open and begins to unfold. Meditation points within blossom inwardly, they infold, but open up to entirety as well. Be your own point and don't falter despite the rocky roads.

"Your vision will become clear only when you can look into your own heart. Who looks outside, dreams; who looks inside, awakes." ~Carl Jung

"Now, Kalamas, don't go by reports, by legends, by traditions, by scripture, by logical conjecture, by inference, by analogies, by agreement through pondering views, by probability, or by the thought, 'This contemplative is our teacher.' When you know for yourselves that,

'These qualities are skillful; these qualities are blameless; these qualities are praised by the wise; these qualities, when adopted & carried out, lead to welfare & to happiness' - then you should enter & remain in them. ~Buddha

  Be your point. Be your own teacher and seek guidance inwardly. After, that is, your vision becomes clear, after that is you break some shells and understand the form and flow of life and yourself. This is the very concept behind intuition, in and tuition mean inner learning. When your vision is clear you gain true insight, wisdom and happiness and can be your own teacher with intuition. Single pointed focus leads to clarity and enables you to be your own teacher. Remember that all it takes is one point to change the situation of entirety, just as a single point of light can shine and light a whole room of darkness.

  Tibetan Buddhists often refer to there being just two types of meditation. The first is concentration meditation or single pointed meditation. The second is contemplation meditation or analytical meditation. Single-pointed meditation develops an elevated focused mind state. When we are focused, absorbed in concentration, we can reap rewards for all kinds of secular activities, but more valuably we can then analyze our thinking and being and come to great understandings of our mind, and of our true nature. The benefits of being focused are remarkable in and of themselves, however the major spiritual and psychological breakthroughs happen after single-pointed meditation when a higher state of concentration is developed and harnessed. After single-pointed meditation practice we can then have higher insightful and intuitive learning experiences and awakenings through contemplative analysis.

Recitation of mantras, or focusing on a single idea or word are both examples of single-pointed meditation that enables us to then go further inward or into a subject. Non-dualistic single-pointed meditation develops the ability to have further high minded insights. Nine stages of single-pointedness are extrapolated to be utilized for gaining and maintaining the meditative focus that enhances the capability of further high level analyzation.

1) inwardly placing the mind on the object

2) extending the duration of the concentration

3) replacing the mind on the object when it is distracted

4) continuously restoring the focus of the mind

5) achieving a state of inner control

6) achieving a state of inner pacification

7) achieving a state of complete inner peace

8) achieving single-pointed mind

9) achieving mental equilibrium

Achievement of single-pointed concentration is followed by mental equilibrium in the set of nine ways of abiding or nine ways of resting the mind. Each of these nine thoughts enables the control needed to hone and calm our thinking. This achievement of mental equilibrium suggests that there is then multiplicity, at least more than one, for equilibrium is always between multiples, balance potentially between the left and right side of the brain, between positive and negative, between masculine and feminine nature, and balance of our gut and mind via the heart center.

Balance can be achieved through single-pointed focus. This idea of the power of focus is illustrated in the yoga idea of drishti. When practicing yoga asanas or positions it is important to focus the gaze on a point. Sometimes the points maybe body parts or sometimes a still point ahead beyond you. The more difficult the position the more important the single-pointed focus of the gaze becomes. And the more the drishti practice is utilized the more balanced one becomes.

Each asana has a specific drishti, of which there are nine; the tip of the nose, the toes, the fingertips, the thumb, the navel, the inner eye or third eye, up to the sky, to the right, and to the left.

The drishti focus of our eyes results in physical balance and is applicable to our mental balance and concentration as well. Focus of our gaze enables higher concentration potential generally speaking. Utilizing drishti concentration of our inner eye, enables the balance of our mind state, just as focusing our sight enables our physical balance. The focus of our inner sight on a single point or action, or a single state of being, be it real or imaginary, be it incomprehensibly huge or inconceivably tiny single point in space and time vastly improves our potential concentration.

Enhanced concentration enables our ability to accomplish the position at hand and ultimately an increased ability to accomplish future tasks and positions. The more physically and mentally focused we are the more balance we are capable of maintaining, even in difficult positions, and the more capable we become.

In yoga this enhancement and refinement of mind through the practice of drishti, soft focus gaze, is called ekagra. Ekagra is a soft focused gaze of intent with the mind or third eye on a single thinking principle. Simply practicing focusing the gaze and our intent is directly beneficial in all meditations and secular activities as well and the indirect long term benefits can be remarkable. High levels of concentration enable the individual to remain steady and little swayed by the distractions and delusions of the mind that otherwise tend to come up.

Meditation can be done with the eyes open, though often visual stimulation leads to distraction, as does stimulation of any of the senses, so the eyes are normally closed. It is of course beneficial to at least experience meditation with the eyes open in a relaxed but intently focused manner. A candle can be utilized, or on object with spiritual value can be used or a random crease on the wall in front of you.

Bodhidharma, who is most well-known for bringing martial arts to China as the story goes, famously meditated by staring at a cave wall for years. One story goes he tore his eyelashes off to stay awake longer and stare at a point on the wall. Meditation on the point builds concentration for any number of activities while enhancing clarity.

"Not creating delusions is enlightenment." ~Bodhidharma

If you have meditation practitioner friends eyegazing is an extremely powerful process. Exchanging gaze with others, focusing your gaze into the gaze of another while also utilizing meditative breathing is extremely rewarding. Perhaps eyegazing develops empathy for others while at the same time demanding a certain level of sureness and centeredness in oneself to stare into the eyes of another and this combination helps regain our heart center.

There is the expression that the eyes are the windows into the soul. When the situation is right windows are like mirrors. If you place mirrors opposite one another there is a reflection and projection into near infinity. The effects of two people eyegazing can be like two mirrors facing each other, the meditation effects can be potentiated in powerful manners, as if near infinitely.

Their Points

"Once upon a time there was a monkey who was very fond of cherries. One day he saw a delicious-looking cherry, and came down from his tree to get it. But the fruit turned out to be in a clear glass bottle. After some experimentation, the monkey found that he could get hold of the cherry by putting his hand into the bottle by way of the neck. As soon as he had done so, he closed his hand over the cherry; but then he found that he could not withdraw his fist holding the cherry, because it was larger than the internal dimension of the neck. Now all this was deliberate, because the cherry in the bottle was a trap laid by a monkey-hunter who knew how monkeys think. The hunter, hearing the monkey's whimperings, came along and the monkey tried to run away. But, because his hand was, as he thought, stuck in the bottle, he could not move fast enough to escape. But, as he thought, he still had hold of the cherry. The hunter picked him up. A moment later he tapped the monkey sharply on the elbow, making him suddenly relax his hold on the fruit. The monkey was free, but he was captured. The hunter had used the cherry and the bottle, but he still had them." ~Idries Shah

On geometrical metaphysical examination of the caught monkey parable we see that the cherry is another's point set in a bottle and the bottle is a solid capable of holding volume, which traps the monkey, or the monkey mind. The hunter puts his point into the solid and the monkey mind succumbs to the trap. The monkey mind is the endlessly pursuing mind, a monkey swinging from thought to ego filled unconscious thought, as if vines.

   The lesson within this parable is to not get caught up by the points of others set upon certain solids. To do so remain gently still and stable instead of being convinced to always hold on to one vine or another, vines being like lines of energy and linear thinking. Be on point instead of holding on to another's point or swinging back and forth as if on vines.

"Just as a monkey swinging through the trees grabs one branch and lets it go only to seize another, so too, that which is called thought, mind or consciousness arises and disappears continually both day and night."
~Buddha

   Instead of feeding the ruffian monkey mind within, Buddha suggested to be like a gentle deer, on point, but gently so. If you can shake off something that you ardently hold onto, like a monkey holds the cherry in the bottle, than you are gaining enlightenment, if not you gain entanglement. The same goes for letting go of someone else's point, their focus tangibly actualized, on the collective conscious or your consciousness. The adoption of a corporate identity label on your lapel and wearing it out of work is an instance of wearing someone else's point. A worse example is becoming reactionary because of someone else's drama, reactionary as an actor in their play.

Many buttons or triggers basically cause disconnection with our true nature, with the present, and misdirect our power potential. One of the best ways to clear your sight and hearing toward intuitive comprehension and higher meditative mind states is to address and thereby decompress the buttons and triggers we have. By addressing them we make them inoperable, no longer optional. Where there was once a button is instead just smooth comprehension without knobs poking out, calling out to be pushed.

When we are capable of recognizing our center point and being centered we will not be thrown off our power by the points of others. When we know ourselves and we know our hearts, by heart, that is completely and openly, then we know we can remain focused despite the influence of others and outside circumstances.

Sometimes some people will do all they can to make other people recognize and value their point. Their point may be decent enough and it may be a cherry in a bottle to trap the monkey minded. We often have intense desire to hold onto things, to points that are ideas and points that are figurative cherries. As we age and as things change we focus our desire on different points. When we realize that some points might be representative of genuine authenticity, of individualized and individuated truth, and others might be make believe, completely fake articles for misdirection away from the authenticity of self and others, we can better discern what is worth holding onto.

Usually there are many personal reasons for those who hold onto an inauthentic point, but it often enough might come down to the simple fact that they do not want to break through the shells encasing their true nature as if such is grasped around their entirety. The mind and ego go to great lengths to maintain comfort and control, no matter if it's not the best outcome for us.

We all go through great lengths to hold onto our point and get our point across and sometimes we'll end up crossing over and crossing out another's point in doing so, rather than making connection. Sometimes without realizing it we may be so adamant about a point we don't see the big picture.

When I was inspired or more implored to write this book I had just left California to embark on a continental book tour. I, like any writer I suppose, have untapped reservoirs of hope rooted in the conviction that ideas can change the world, so I left the mountains, my friends and everything I've known for many years in a van packed with only the most basic sustenance; food, books and my adorable dog.

Traveling at all, and driving across the country especially, offers a unique observation point into society's wells and ills. And from this new liberating perspective, as an outside observer, it was apparent that we have essentially become a culture based on practices of separation. We collectively try to separate ourselves from the rest of the collective, the drama and trauma, but in doing so we separate ourselves from the love and our own true nature.

The more open we are to others, or to god, or godliness, or whatever, the more open we are energy. It's really that simple. And most of us mostly are holding onto a point, trying to get our point across and we'll cross over whomever in the process, oblivious to all else.

No matter where I go, I focus on first seeing the gold in everyone, their divine spark. I acknowledge and greet people I see and I have met some of the most beautiful people just by being open in this way. I focus on seeing gold in people and it is extracted, not always, but frequently. Everyone has golden shine in them, personal alchemy can extract it, transforming their lead to gold, their density to light, their clenched hand into an open one.

If we are divided, we are conquered. If we consider ourselves separated from our community (great and small) and from our natural environment, our outer state as well as our inner state, we lose the empowerment that communication, and that connection provides.

The power of communication in any manner is enormous; words have the power to change the world, and personal exchanges are the most resonating form of communication. Nothing is more powerful than looking another human in the eyes and speaking, and hearing, truth.

"If a man is not faithful to his own individuality, he cannot be loyal to anything." ~Claude McKay, writer and poet

All institutions lean toward empowering themselves, and other institutions, and disempowering the individuals that are under, away from their wing. The individuals within institutions act as the institution they are under; they do not think as individuals, perform as individuals, or develop as individuals. Rather, they succumb to the cherry trap, fall for the point of another, working for the benefit of institutional illusions, paid to leave their humanity at the door.

To put it simply, if you are not training, you're being trained. If you are acting on behalf of the institutional point more often than acting on behalf of your unique individual impulse, you begin to lose yourself and your true nature. If you constantly hold onto the point of another you're never yourself.

We have so many things to hold onto in life. And so many of their points captivate us, but rarely are we captivated with our own points. Today so many people hold on to their cellular devices so frequently they are indeed never on point, their point. In order to be on point we have to let it go. Let go of whatever you are holding onto, be it literally a cellular device or otherwise a constructed idea.

The Hopi People of Arizona eloquently described this predicament when they encountered institutionalized individuals for the first time. They referred to the institutionalized Europeans who arrived on their shores as 'two hearted'. They recognized their greed and ego, their lost conscious connection due a second 'heart' to feed that could never be satisfied; a cold empty heart that devoured everything before it; an institutional heart, which constantly seeks, but never finds fulfilment in the 'masculine' ideals of power, conformity, nationalism, and war while forsaking the 'feminine' virtues of sustainability, individuality, co-operation and nurturing.

The singularity of the heart center is extremely important and requires a lot of work to remove attachments and to be in. To begin to be in your center, do not act on behalf of machines, do not lend your heart, your truth, to speak on institutional points.

Because of two-heartedness, there is division, and lacking authenticity. We live in a sea of pollution and systemic corruption and a monolithic culture of separation, where we yield to institutions and afford them the divine right of kings to get their point across. We are born believing we are indebted to manmade structures, and spend our lives paying others for the privilege of life itself, with our hand stuck in the bottle.

The personal alchemy of individuation in meditation is the sole domain of individuals, for individuals. It is tremendously difficult to step away from the mediation and control of institutions, but it is possible. It starts by ceasing your support for the status quo and living your truth without compromise. Individuation sprouts from meditation, and meditation overrides mediation.

In order to live as an individual, according only to your own personal alchemy, choose practices which fulfil your heart and promote self-development. Practice tai chi chaun, yoga, simple breath work and most importantly meditation. Practice your art. Practice singing and dancing. Practice stepping out of line, confronting institutional thinking, and speaking your truth. Practice being open and nonjudgmental with everyone around you. Practice being unified with your heart, authentically open to the experiences and energies life offers. Take your meditation conceptualizations into the world.

"Only by discovering alchemy have I clearly understood that the unconscious is a process and that ego's rapports with the unconscious and his contents initiate an evolution, more precisely a real metamorphoses of the psyche." ~Carl Jung

To see the authenticity in others we must be authentic ourselves. Practice seeing the gold within people, and looking beyond their conditioned disconnected behaviors. And practice questioning your own disconnected behaviors when, or should I say, as they arise. See others as their authentic golden self, in their truth, not just as they would have you see them. And visualize you in your golden authenticity. Through the power of communication, individuality and human connection, we will reclaim our true nature, our point, and create a future that values life, not just lifeless social machinery, their points.

When we initiate turning lead ideas into golden points we are soon able to do it within ourselves and others. If we accept people for their initial representation we may get the wrong idea, when we see them authentically we can transmute their dense dull facade to one that is more authentic and lighter.

Sometimes all we have to do is let it go. People can be like dogs with points of contention. We might do this all in our own head or in reality. The point is often like a bone and nobody wants it until someone else does, and then everyone becomes convinced they want it so much it's worth injury to obtain, or wasting time to ponder.

When we just let it go, situations diffuse, the hunter fails. The same applies for when someone has a bone to pick with you. If we simply let it go, then they'll just move along. The same goes for a contentious thought. If we don't take issue with the point then there is no contention, but if we hold onto something that necessitates confrontation then there's reason to fight over, what really amounts to, bones. Monkeys and dogs cannot easily let points go, consciousness has the distinct ability to let it go.

The Lines

"There is geometry in the humming of the strings, there is music in the spacing of the spheres." ~Pythagoras

First there is a point symbolic for clear concentration. The second geometrical dimension is a line. The line symbolizes connection. The second form and flow is a line, manifest from points. Sometimes lines can manifest from letting go and moving on. There are a number of correlating esoteric and mathematic principles on lines. Lines can be seen as dividing lines, or as connecting lines, often one and the same, their differences based simply on perspective.

   Geometric chords, from the Latin chorda, meaning bowstring, follow the same principles as energy lines. Geometric chords can be positive or negative. They can link any point to any point infinitely and as the bowstring implies, they become a taking off point. The same goes with linear energy. Lines represent connections which might be positive or negative and might connect infinitely or divide in one way or another, positively or negatively, often simply depending on perspective.

   It is important, in life and meditation, to bend, but it is also equally or more important to hold steadfast as you bend. Trees that are stiff tend to snap, trees that are not rooted blow over. Trees that are strongly rooted and yet bend can stand the winds of change, the forms and flows of outer influences. In life, and in practice, think of the tree analogy to find sturdy balance.

As far as energy and meditation techniques, concentrating on energy lines are not abstractly instructed among many meditation techniques. Tibetan meditation traditions speak of energy cords, as do Daoist meditation techniques, perhaps each rooted (pun intended) in traditional understandings from India. Many practices have a single divine cord, some use multiple cords, such as golden and silver cords together, or cords of differing colors. Many imagine a cord connecting self to the North Star, the one unmoving star in the sky, and another connecting to Mother Earth.

The simplest linear connection meditation uses essentially two lines. Imagine one line linking your center point from you crown chakra at the crown of your head to energy above, The Sun or The North Star are frequently used. Imagine another from your root chakra at your tailbone linking your center point to the earth below. Imagine connection with above and below. Eventually the lines are integrated, the two energies connect within in an intersecting loop.

The main beginning idea or focus here is to connect with and then eventually integrate the contrasting energies of the earthly and universal, of the divine feminine and the divine masculine. The Earth energy connects with the universal energy and links us to the contrasting watery energy of Earth and electrical energy of the universe, the sturdy gravity with the electric ethereal.

Points and lines are generally masculine and planes and solids are generally feminine. Masculine energy is direct and focused on purpose like the point. Masculine energy is about action and direction like proceeding from A to B, like lines. Feminine energy is free flowing and circulating like circles. Feminine energy is about emotion including limitless love, akin to all-encompassing spheres.

With linear connection we can imagine and bring our attention to being grounded. One of the simplest and most profound tai chi meditations essentially stands still and upright and imagine connection to Earth. There are many variations of forms of standing meditations, but the flow of connection is the main theme. Often called the Universal Pillar simple stillness standing meditations, while embodying tai chi principles including relaxation, are profoundly powerful. Energy is exchanged through grounding with the Earth.

When we are grounded we are balanced, when we are balanced we are potentiated. In our culture of separation most are imbalanced, and altogether disconnected to Mother Earth.

The most difficult function most everyone ever does is to learn to use language; to learn how to communicate thoughts, feelings and ideas into sounds. The complex nuances of communication are the most difficult things we learn as humans, and also the most powerful and important tool we have for individuation, in part by way of clearing the occasional misdirection we've adopted as part of our language and thinking.

Indeed, what and how we communicate and what and how we imagine have the power to change the world. Just as importantly, language and its transformation over time reveals a lot about our collective consciousness.

Ma is the primal tone of the divine feminine according to Hindu and Buddhist ideas. It is also, essentially, what most of us call our mothers.

English: Mama/Mum, Afrikaans: Ma, Portugese: Mãe, Dutch: Moer, Greek: Màna, Russian: Mat', Hindi: Maji, Romanian: Maica, Italian: Madre, Yiddish: Muter, French: mère, Polish: Matka, Punjabi: Mai, Serbian: Majka, Albanian: Mëmë, Haitian: Manman, Slovenian: Máti,

Mandarin: Mǔqīn, Zulu: Umama, Sicilian: Matri, Spanish: Madre,

Icelandic: móðir, Swahili: Mzaa, Vietnamese: mẹ, Swedish: Morsa, Thai: Mæ̀, Nepali: Āmā, Tamil: Am'mā

While 'ma' is commonly the root of "mother" in so many curiously disparate cultures around the world, another variation of mother also echoes the sacred Aum. In Hinduism, Aum is the sound of the original vibration of consciousness; of god manifested in form. The sacred linguistic roots of our words for mother tell us a lot about the reverential roots of our ancestral societies. The divine feminine represents motherly compassionate nurturing.

It is no secret that the feminine nature of our collective consciousness has been unnaturally diminished. As our reverence for the feminine has diminished, so too has the influence of women on civilization. At the same time masculinity has been distorted. Around the world, people have lost their energetic balance, becoming overtly militant, punitive, competitive, nationalistic and institutionalized. This energetic imbalance has led to institutions operating in such a way to disregard feminine virtues, such as individualism, cooperation and sustainability.

This imbalance is clearly reflected in, and perpetuated by, our use of language. Our distorted perceptions of masculine and feminine are evidenced in the way we use the words 'manly' and 'womanly' and our descriptions generally.

The oppression of the feminine is further obvious when we look at the psychology behind the systemic environmental destruction of Mother Earth and the mistreatment of women globally. The sacred feminine once kept whole communities intuitively in tune with Earth Mother, valuing her as the nurturer of life, and honoring her need to be nurtured in return. By perceiving disconnection from their natural environment and the energy she embodies, society undervalues the need for sustainable, compassionate thinking, and institutes consent to destroy great swathes of our beautiful planet in the name of institutional progress.

"I admit thoughts influence the body." ~Albert Einstein

Our over-developed egos, and our denatured vision of Earth Mother results in the inability to sense the sacredness of nature and with nature, the feminine. Our egos cause separation, we don't feel nor seek connection to the web of creation, the network of life on Earth.

Believing we are disconnected from our environment and each other, our unbalanced decision makers steer an unbalanced society toward destructive practices. Meditation seeks to make connection and balance. Those who have lost the essence of who they really are cannot function in a harmonious and balanced manner, let alone at a high-vibrational level. Without balance of masculine and feminine, the yin and yang, a radical warring perversion results.

If the divine feminine was truly celebrated, revered and embodied, and if the true nature of the divine masculine was embodied, our society would be shaped by quite a different balance of interests.

The distorted expression of the masculine within our institutional structures and the desecration of the feminine, as constructed by those institutional powers, are evidenced by the rather un-divine expressions of masculinity and femininity. The heroes and heroine archetypes serve to steer the collective toward accepting constant distortion of the masculine and feminine, and to engage in the roles these archetypes embody; the passive beauty and the unfeeling warrior.

In order to best overcome mediation we can use the power of our own words and our consciousness. To initiate inner and outer balance of the masculine and feminine orientations we have to bring about even connection.

"Whereas logic and objectivity are usually the predominant features of a man's outer attitude, or are at least regarded as ideals, in the case of a woman it is feeling. But in the soul it is the other way round: inwardly it is the man who feels, and the woman who reflects." ~Carl Jung

Carl Jung proposed there are four stages of development of the anima and animus. These are our inner femininity and masculinity. Eve, Helen, Mary and Sophia are used to illustrate the anima. Man of mere physical power, Man of action or romance, Man as a professor or clergyman and Man as a helpful guide are used to understand the animus. The characteristic descriptions can be used to heighten and refine your understanding of, and connection to the divine masculine and divine feminine.

Throughout recorded time, the power of consciousness and conscious words to change things, to change everything, remains a constant. One word or phrase is all it takes to change form and flow. This is arguably why censorship has constantly been enacted against individuals who express ideas - through words - that challenge our unconscious acceptance of what reality is. What is your phrase to build divinity within and without?

To heal ourselves and a world increasingly ravaged by unchecked greed, we must rediscover the honor of the sacred masculine and value equally the qualities of the divine feminine - a devotion to Mother Earth, ecology, sustainability, peace to all beings. The future of our civilization now depends on our willingness to embody and revere the energy of the feminine and the masculine, in conscious balance, in our words and our deeds. In order to balance the form and flow of the divine feminine and divine masculine think of the masculine as the river rock and the feminine as the river. The masculine is structural and logical, the feminine is integral and loving. The masculine riverbed is always there to support the waters that flow onward.

When we meditatively connect to the divine feminine and divine masculine we are grounded and yet suspended, we nurture and are nurtured, protect and are protected. The linear connection with above and below is not simply a connection with our masculine and feminine selves and, but a divine connection with divine masculine and divine feminine natures. This connection is built as a process, literally through repeated practice, repeated engagement of relaxed awareness to the point that the repetition develops spiritual friction resulting in spiritual flame. This is why Tibetan Buddhist monks for instance will do so many X thousand prostrations, and why various practitioners perform many dedications of sorts, to enhance their state of being, their notion of dedication. Any number of extremes are often required in correspondence with great lessons of all sorts, in order to enhance the emotion of dedication and focus.

The biblical story of Jacob's ladder describes Jacob using his imagination to form a meditative connection with the heavens above. It is not so subtly an instruction to meditate at night and use your imagination to instigate the chi movement in energy lines.

"11 And he lighted upon a certain place, and tarried there all night, because the sun was set; and he took of the stones of that place, and put them for his pillows, and lay down in that place to sleep. 12 And he dreamed, and behold a ladder set up on the earth, and the top of it reached to heaven: and behold the angels of God ascending and descending on it. 13 And, behold, the Lord stood above it, and said, I am the Lord God of Abraham thy father, and the God of Isaac: the land whereon thou liest, to thee will I give it, and to thy seed; 14 And thy seed shall be as the dust of the earth, and thou shalt spread abroad to the west, and to the east, and to the north, and to the south: and in thee and in thy seed shall all the families of the earth be blessed. 15 And, behold, I am with thee, and will keep thee in all places whither thou goest, and will bring thee again into this land; for I will not leave thee, until I have done that which I have spoken to thee of. 16 And Jacob awaked out of his sleep, and he said, Surely the Lord is in this place; and I knew it not. 17 And he was afraid, and said, How dreadful is this place! this is none other but the house of God, and this is the gate of heaven. 18 And Jacob rose up early in the morning, and took the stone that he had put for his pillows, and set it up for a pillar, and poured oil upon the top of it." ~Genesis 28:11 -28:18

Jacob's ladder has the four dimensions of geometry in it. The ladder is the focus, it being an obvious metaphoric relation to a line, or linear energy flow. The rock and seeds bear resemblance to points as does the dust of the earth concept. The gate is like a plane and the house is a solid enclosure of space. The whole idea is about mixing and intermingling energies to achieve balance and what might be called enhanced vibration. This is expressed in the angels of God ascending and descending the ladder.

If you ever feel as if you cannot handle a situation, or find the answer to a question on your own, ask for connection with your guiding angels or you own personal higher self or creator (God). When connection with your angels occurs at just the right angle, with just the right intention, magic can occur, or to put it another way, when you angle yourself to higher thinking elevated situations occur by way of your imagination and meditation. When our heart is in the right place and placed right we are able to linearly connect with angels descending and descending. When our hearts are in the right place and placed right we can help ourselves and help others as an angel at just the right angle.

Most every meditation has the quality of releasing tension and then unifying divine masculine and divine feminine energies. The secretive Freemasonic symbol of the compass and square together, often presented with a central G, represent the generative qualities that bringing masculine and feminine energies together results in. The G is said to stand for god, or geometry, or generative, or gnosis, and all these things and more. The idea of simply running energy, or grounding, is reflective of this, where we essentially connect with above and below, the masculine and feminine, and imagine releasing and receiving energy, so as to improve our clarity. The feelings and tangible results of meditation and intermingling of, or running energies are profoundly spiritual but not yet limited to religious order, in my experience.

[22]. Jesus saw some children who were taking the breast: he said to his disciples: "These little ones who suck are like those who enter the Kingdom." They said to him: "If we are little, shall we enter the Kingdom?" Jesus says to them: "When you make the two <become> one, and when you make the inside like the outside and the outside like the inside, and the upper like the lower! And if you make the male and female one, so that the male is no longer male and the female no longer female, and when you put eyes in the place of an eye, and a hand in the place of a hand, and a foot in the place of a foot, and an image in the place of an image, then you will enter [the Kingdom!"]
~Gospel of Thomas

The Violet flame meditation is one of the most widely celebrated meditations and contains linear systems similar in design to the idea of linear connection with higher energy. In this practice, what is essentially a violet flaming laser is developed with higher source which connects through our violet or purple crown chakra, opening our receptive capability as well as our capability of giving.

Tai chi and related meditation theory direct one to think about being attached to mother earth, grounded through your feet physically and through your tailbone metaphysically, and the North Star suspending us or connecting us via a golden cord to our crown chakra from above. Tai chi practitioners and martial artists develop the idea that they have a linear connection to the ground from their tailbone, often called a dragon tail, a line that roots them and propels them connected to the Earth, along with their feet as well as linear connection to the above.

The legs serve as linear grounding lines in many ways. Our feet serve to connect us, to assist us in being grounded. The most overlooked chakras, or energy points, are what called the bubbling spring wells among tai chi and chi gung practitioners. These points serve to connect us with the Earth, to release and intake energy. The points are located just underneath the balls of the feet. Every chakra is a point, connected by nadis, or lines. When we practice individuation and are healthful we can project and detect planes or fields of thought and emotion. When we reach higher stages of meditation and individuation we can create our own volume, become capable of holding space, through the manifesting power of love. Chakras are energy points of intersect, nadis are energy lines, projected and detected thoughts are energy planes, and love, being in love, living in compassionate loving balance, is the solid.

Individuation is beautiful because it is about your development, your spirituality and/or mentality, not the development of a religious formation or institutionalization whatsoever. When grounding with mother earth and connecting with father sky you can individuate in any fashion that suits you. If you are in the mountains you might feel like tree roots grounding you or lighting connecting you, or if on the coast you might imagine other connections like seaweed for instance. The point is to engage the linear flow up and down the length of the spine, and to initiate the exchange of divine masculine and divine feminine energy.

The more you learn about chakra characteristics the better for the following practice, but your intuitive understanding about your own personal relation to guttural, mental and heart focus functioning as related to yourself are enough for its productivity. Imagine being there as you meditate linearly, literally being in the deep gut, heart, mind, or the depths of earth and heights of the universe. Imagine being in a chakra and feeling it out and opening it up.

Lines are not so subtly depicted in the symbol of the rod and serpents, including The Staff of Hermes, The Caduceus and The Rod of Asclepius. The symbol now is synonymous with medical care, because of the regeneration ideas snakes have, and not so subtly because it is basically a microcosmic reflection of our DNA strands. Its understanding metaphysically, or macrocosmically, is our spine as a straight staff of office (our vertical individual energetic consciousness) that the winged serpents (wavy lines of countering oppositional energies) ascend, as demonstrated in yoga philosophy as the opening of the lunar Ida and solar Pingala channels along the spine.

"You have to keep breaking your heart until it opens." ~Rumi

Speaking further esoterically or secretively, the serpents further correspond to the serpent like energies that open our shell from the inside up, rising from the Earth or our earthen energies, moving through dense negativity holding us back so as to return to clarity as if opening a rift to access energy, where there was formerly only density and closure.

If the idea of a rift opening is frightening consider the all-around darkness otherwise, enclosing in on and wrapping around you preventing you from becoming you, whether experiential or otherwise. The above symbols are related to how we can either ascend in meditation or descend through meditation usually having to do with monetization, the materialistic as opposed to the meditative. In this way we can see how wavy linear flows, as illustrated here, can either assist us, releasing us, or coil around us, entangling us to attachments further. Focus on empowering lines, on balancing oppositional forms and flows, so that they are freeing rather than entangling.

As an alternate or accompanying thought, focus on a time when you connected people or energy together in some manner simply by knowing something or feeling something and sharing. Imagine such linear connections in nature, like trees and all sorts of plants being rooted to the earth and reaching for connection with sunlight, particles and waves.

Imagine other lines in nature, like lightning which is normally preceded by and accompanied by raindrops. Imagine your linear connections as powerful and flowing like lightning but constant like great trees. Imagine the geometry in the strings that weave everything together.

Cutting Cords

"Logic will get you from A to B. Imagination will take you everywhere."
~Albert Einstein

Sometimes, if we become tricked or convinced that we don't know the answer to a problem, the solution is found in our imagination. Sometimes all we need to do is enact the power of imagination to thwart or cut constricting cords which attach us to places or states of consciousness that are no longer positive. Sometimes all we need to do is shift our understanding to change our situation, our pattern. Just as sometimes we believe we cannot perceive energy, sometimes we also believe that we cannot change our energy. Sometimes to perceive energy, this is especially accurate with internal chi, we need to imagine it first and then it cannot be imagined away. The same goes for cutting negative ties bonding you or holding you down, first imagine the ability to shake off the constructs, imagine they are removed, then think through and feel the negativity removed.

Think about someone who holds power over you in a negative manner, in a manner so subtle that to explain it would take a long back story, or perhaps in a manner so strong that you don't want to talk about it, and imagine cutting or removing their etheric cords and connections to you. Imagine the cords between family and friends that may need some clearing or cleaning to be like arterial connections. If there is negative dense sludge and experiential trauma that may have clogged the walls and soured the wells imagine it clean and clear, if they are to remain.

If you have ever spent time with and walked with different dogs on a leash you will see that some dogs understand the leash they are attached to and some do not, some dogs will figure out ways to undo and bite through their rope, their cord, some will learn to deal with it or even untangle themselves when tangling occurs. Some learn the special limits allowed by the cord, some dogs easily become entangled and do not know what to do, how to approach the dilemma and some would rather chew through anything including themselves, to get from out the cords. Some dogs might even strangle themselves in their entanglement brought on from being frantic about the cord or leash.

Humans may exist in this state like the tied up dog for long periods of time. Some of us are aware of the leash or the many ropes and cords attached to us, so we easily maneuver around, some of us are not, and trip over our own karmic bonds repeatedly or trap ourselves in entanglement to the point of strangulation. We are spiritually bonded, tied to and attached via ethereal cords to certain people, places and things, especially it seems, to people. These relationships and attachments sometimes offer us loving strength, but because emotional input is often a requirement to spiritually make the ties, and because emotions often are based in negative fear based feelings, the cords are also often enough negative or rotted as opposed to rooted and vibrant. The best way to cut or cleanse the cords is to meditate and become aware of the passing thoughts. We allow the thoughts to arise and we address them, and then we move on, let the thoughts pass and not coalesce into thick emotions.

A powerful meditation on its own is called, or can be summed up as, grounding. Grounding uses energy cords for connection. In this practice you simply imagine that excess energy is being diffused from out your dragon tail, or energy grounding cord that connects to the Earth via your root chakra or from your spine and through your tailbone. Grounding allows you to recycle energy that is not your own into the earth but stuck to you or around you and at the same time access higher quality energy, a giving and receiving, or releasing and obtaining. The grounding cord is followed by a cord to connect us, or ground us, to the above. Many teachings say to ground with Earth first, other say the opposite. You may feel that connecting above first is how it works for you. There are all sorts of ways to change it but the point is to move energy. The grounding meditation can remove disturbances that manifest on levels we realize and levels which we are not aware.

What are levels? A specific contemplation which broadens our spectrum of consideration of levels of reality, let alone levels of psychology and physiology, is the Analogy of the Divided Line. Socrates divided information into four parts. Socrates noted there is the tangible, like a tree (DE) and there are reflections of the tangible (CD), like a tree's reflection in a pond. There is also the intangible like numbers (BC) and finally the smallest portion is the reflections of the intangible (AB), algebraic equations for instance.

The formation is illustrative of how there are levels to reality and that they increase in their subtlety. The line is often placed horizontally, but when we place it vertically this ascension of sensitivity becomes clearer. The largest part of the set is the tangible and the smallest, most elusive part is the reflections of the intangible, or subtle energy. Consideration of The Divided Line expands awareness and initiates consciousness. The Divided Line can also be useful when seeking to sense energy. Use it to conceptualize people, place and thing through the four formats.

The formation I call the duality of polarity of information also contributes to our awareness of subtleties and subtle energies, and also inspires attuned attention. There are four types of information; known knowns, known unknowns, unknown unknowns and unknown knowns. There are many aspects of reality that are so subtle extreme sensitivity is required to be aware of them, such as the cords which might be attached to us.

"There are things known and there are things unknown, and in between are the doors of perception."~ Aldous Huxley

We usually have cords attached to us from traumatic experiences perpetuated on us during childhood traumas, childhood insults and injuries, although all sorts of experiences at any time with people who present us with situations with strings attached can cause such cords to entangle. Mostly cords occur between people we have close 'ties' to. We can even have negative ties to things we yield power to, have a web of ego centric materialism is the most frequent imbalance. The best way to cut past these traumas which lead to negative storylines played or re acted over and over, negative behavior repetitions, is to ask yourself, really pursue in depth, why you behave in certain ways. When we deeply consciously question our perceptions and actions, so deeply we get to the very roots of the trained thinking which may be problematic by one degree or another.

When cutting cords is difficult, approach the situational draining with a new reality, make a shift in your perception. If the problem is essentially a belief that you are not good enough, shift it to believing that you're so great that whatever you thought you were not good enough for, change it to being not good enough for you. If you are operating with the cord of another on you, trying to pull you down realize that they simply do not want you to use to your full potential, become your true nature, because they are intimidated by you and anyone who would be in their true nature around them. Many people culturally would rather inhibit than uplift, hinder rather than help, but you can break that chain and their chains which train them to be this way and suggest that it's acceptable for others to be this way too.

"Care about what other people think and you will always be their prisoner." ~Lao Tzu

When you feel as if you are dealing with too much energy or energy that is not your own, imagine that you return the excess energy back to earth where it can be recycled back into quality and useful energy by Mother Earth energy. While connecting and grounding out negative energy through your dragon tail or grounding cord, imagine that positive, universal energy is coming in through your head and assisting in the process. Quality positive energy can be obtained in this way however mostly all we need to do to obtain positive energy is relieve ourselves of the negativity, which grounding assists in.

"Is the universe eternal? Or not? Or both? Or neither? Is the universe finite? Or not? Or both? Or neither? Is the self identical with the body? Or is the self different from the body? Does the Tathagata (name Buddha used for himself meaning the one who has thus come and the one who has thus gone) exist after death? Or not? Or both? Or neither?" ~The Fourteen Unanswered Questions of Buddha.

The theories of special relativity and general relativity, as theorized by Albert Einstein, in part state that reality is four dimensional, made up of time, length, width and depth. With this in mind we are capable of questioning everything in four dimensional terms. This questioning through physics originally applied to physical objects can also be applied to energetic concepts.

There are a few questions which people have posed since time immemorial, like those posed to and unanswered by Buddha. They reveal our nature to question everything, even the unanswerable about the end and beginning of lines, of form and flow.

The Fourteen questions are actually four questions, three with four aspects and one with two. Despite Buddha's refusal to answer the questions they were still posed in the most developed manner possible in hopes of obtaining an answer.

Buddha believed people existed in either two states; in existence or nonexistence. It is believed he thought the imponderables could never truly be answered and that they led to states of negativity and nonexistence, ultimately inconsequential to our earthly predicament of eliminating suffering and attaining enlightenment.

Questions are posed completely in four ways, as illustrated in the formation of the imponderables. Is it so? Is it not so? Is it both? Is it neither?

There is also the similar thesis, antithesis, synthesis triad. It is often attributed to Georg Wilhelm Hegel, however he criticized what is now called The Hegelian Dialectic. Johann Gottlieb Fichte actually formed the original presentation. Hegel is known to have called the triad of thesis, antithesis and synthesis 'boring' and a 'lifeless schema.' Without nullisis, that is to say without neither, the unlimited alternative, the triad is a lifeless schema.

Hegel did note a similar extrapolation of three; immediate, mediated and concrete. Critics note this trinity to be limited by way of assumptions and errors, soup in what is assumed to be concrete. Nullisis is needed. Nullisis is the distinct and developed fourth philosophical part which often goes unconsidered. No is powerful word which often goes unused.

If mathematics can be considered beautiful, nullisis is beautifully illustrated through the most mysterious and elusive of all arithmetic equations, an imponderable of sorts on its own. It is represented in one of the most mysterious equations of the most complicated of all numbers; zero. Zero represents uncertainty, uncertainty similar to that of the unlimited alternative.

Mathematics seeks clear answers and in practically all arithmetic there are clear answers, but there is only one arithmetic equation that represents uncertainty and unlimited possibility, the nullisis. $0 + 0 = 0$, $0 -- 0 = 0$, $0 \times 0 = 0$, but the answer to 0 divided by 0 is unlimited possibility reflective of nullisis. The answer to zero divided by zero is an undefined unknown. It is the only simple arithmetic equation to which the answer is unknown. A valid answer to this equation could be anything from zero to infinity, just the same as with nullisis the unlimited alternative.

Sometimes we can be caught up in back and forth dynamics that keep us idling in the same question, situation and storyline. When we can put things together in the right manner we can find our answer or find the right way to ask the right questions. There are always other options, other lines we can take. And there are always ways to utilize nullisis in nullification of what seemed like a burden without options.

We do not require the negativity of others to be burdened by cords. We can conjure them on our own. Usually we imagine these restrictions so our ego can be comfortable, sometimes in situations which are not comfortable. We will restrain ourselves from doing things because we have set up our own confines as if we build bars and put ourselves into a cage, or psychological bars that prevent us off from taking certain directions.

Energetic cords or ties are otherwise usually formed with people, places and things that we have some kind of familial or deeply connected roots with. People might be connected by blood, or contract, or experience. We might be attached to places via birth or time spent there, and to things varying with the emotional input into the object and the energy of the object as well. Energetic loops or planes, discussed in next chapter, form bonds or connections via shared ideas or exchanges of concepts and pursuits where there is a giving and receiving form and flow rather than simply an attachment from prior obligations, or experiences.

Tibetan Buddhist illustrations and particularly the following blessing clearly illustrates the differentiation between lines and planes. The following praises includes mention of divine vajra hooks and lassos. When embodying negativity we have to cut the hooks and untie the lassos, when it is positive manifesting energy it can uplift us rather than sink us. This prayer also mentions seeds, potentially for points and the limitless net of illusion for solids or the limitless volume.

"Oṃ āḥ hūṃ hrīḥ! In the palace of power, the blazing of great bliss,

Are the embodiments of the wisdom of discernment, union of bliss and emptiness:

Each on a lotus, its nature bliss free from all attachment,

And the splendor of a great, illuminating vajra sun—

Dharmakāya Amitābha and Vajradharma,

Avalokiteśvara, Lord of the World, the very manifestation of compassion,

Padma Gyalpo, all of saṃsāra and nirvāṇa beneath your control,

Powerful heruka, subjugator of all that appears and exists,

'Secret Wisdom' (Guhyajñāna) and Vajravārāhī,

Döpé Gyalpo, King of Desire, ecstasy supreme, source of the wisdom of great bliss,

Kurukullā, who captivates the mind of every living being without exception,

Masters and mistresses of supreme and ordinary mudrās, dancing in bliss and emptiness,

Hosts of vajra ḍākas and ḍākinīs attract and magnetize.

Remaining always within the state of great equality of appearance and emptiness,

With the dance of your vajra body, you cause the three planes of existence to tremble;

With the sound of your laughter, your unceasing enlightened speech, you draw in the three worlds;

Rays of red light burst out to fill all of saṃsāra and nirvāṇa

And cause the vital essence of conditioned existence and ultimate peace to vibrate and be gathered in.

With your enlightened mind of great vajra passion,

You grant the supreme of all things desired—the two kinds of siddhis;

And with your great vajra hooks and lassoes

You bind the world of appearance and existence in great bliss.

Dancers in the play of the limitless net of illusion,

Who fill space to overflowing, like a vast outpouring of sesame seeds,

Vast array of the Three Roots, hosts of magnetizing deities,

In devotion we pray to you: inspire us with your blessings,

Grant us attainments, ordinary and supreme, and so the siddhi

Of magnetizing, without obstruction, whatever we desire!" ~ Wang Dü: 'The Great Cloud of Blessings'—The Prayer which Magnetizes All that Appears and All that Exists

When we hold onto the lines of others we are living in belief structures. When we believe one thing or another unrealistically, or believe based on a misinterpretation, or because of some lie, or ignorantly and correspondingly ardently, we become as leaves on the tree of another. We are a leaf on someone else's tree or energy line. The best way to cut the cords that influence us to form be leaf structures, is to let them go. Let them all go as if you're your own tree and you're simply letting the leaves fall. Let all the lines you've heard from all the most valued traditions and most trusted institutions go and let all else you hold dear and/or are dearly against go, and be you, if only briefly and occasionally. Form your own line, your own philosophy, theology, theosophy or subject of mastery. If you decide to live as leaf on a tree then you are living in the past. Take what you can from the past, but do not live in it. Otherwise you'll be as the leaf of a tree that grew thousands of years ago, wearing clothes and thinking the thoughts suitable for someone else and some other time far gone.

The Planes

"A human being is a part of the whole called by us universe, a part limited in time and space. He experiences himself, his thoughts and feeling as something separated from the rest, a kind of optical delusion of his consciousness. This delusion is a kind of prison for us, restricting us to our personal desires and to affection for a few persons nearest to us. Our task must be to free ourselves from this prison by widening our circle of compassion to embrace all living creatures and the whole of nature in its beauty." ~Albert Einstein

We begin with a point of concentration. Next is the dimension of connection illustrated by lines. Thirdly we begin energy circulation with loops or wheels. The third stage is expansive and influential and is the dimension of circulation. The lines of connection and the centering point can still be engaged, while the planes or loops then develop circulation. These planes or looping circles cycle energy within us and around us.

The grounding cords, for instance, enhance into loops, and we can cycle energy through our system in many ways. One of the most simple and beneficial ways to exchange and cycles energies can be illustrated utilizing the infinity symbol. The feminine earth energy loops and intersects mingling with the masculine star energy at the root chakra.

Many symbols might contain a meditative element similar to this idea. The cross itself in its numerous variation contains this meditative element. One of the oldest, if not the oldest of all crosses is the ancient Egyptian Ankh. The Ankh symbolizes the masculine and feminine aspects linking together. The feminine (nine) aspect is the circular half above and the masculine (line) is the linear aspect below. The meditative linking and intermingling of the circular feminine and linear masculine energies at the crux point depicted in the Ankh symbolism is said to be a key to represent an energy form and flow that prolong life energy by remaining grounded and circulating energy through the metaphysical body.

There are considered to be 7 main chakra points, like the seven colors we see in a rainbow, but there are many energy points, or spiritual vortexes of and in the body. The nadis, or meridian lines connect these energy points directly metaphysically inside us as well as around us. Circular shaped planes can connect the energy points, chakras, in a spherical counter balanced oppositional flow indirectly and can also potentiate our ability to project and detect among the collective consciousness outside of our physical being. These loops can cycle energy within us and between ourselves and others.

Planes, the third geometrical energy, require a minimum of three points to depict, yet the most optimum shape of a plane is a circle. So while one could think of a plane in three points or more to form a shape, the optimal formation of a plane is circular. Circles offer the most seamless and powerful form and flow and the potential for the simplest and optimum counter rotational oppositional flow with more than one plane. The highest form and flow of a shape or plane is the circle. Use your imagination and attention to circulate energy from one chakra to another. Imagine the counter rotational intersection of another plane or looping energy circulation to move stagnancy. You can experiment in how exactly you connect which chakras in counter rotational loops. If the chakra system is too complex for you currently, simply think about guttural, mental and heart points or layers, and imagine energy circulation flowing through one connections and the other.

In theta healing, a hands off healing practice that focuses on the psychological and more deeply the spiritual nature of diseases and disorders and even misfortune, there are considered to be three molecules we carry through reincarnation; the master cell molecule, the heart molecule and base of spine molecule. These are points of power and potential, where life energy is stored and manifest and from where we can connect with higher and lighter dimensions of energy. These points connect the micro with the macro, the individual with the universal, through potentially higher vibrations of thinking and being. The theory behind the theta healing practice is to be the transistor of creator's energy to allow balance to return by being in tune with higher vibrations. Theta healing allows and assists opening up to higher energy cycles through focusing on being in and cycling a higher vibrational state; theta, as opposed to alpha, beta, gamma and delta.

If you are familiar with the 7 chakras realize that yogis point out that the human system has 84,000 chakras or energy vortex points, each with nadis or linear energy connections circulating our life force throughout. All nadis, of course, flow through and to the heart center. One can form planes or loops between the main chakras or wherever you are physically manifesting pain or discomfort or wherever you feel you need psychological cleansing or spiritual enhancement.

"4 And I looked, and, behold, a whirlwind came out of the north, a great cloud, and a fire infolding itself, and a brightness was about it, and out of the midst thereof as the color of amber, out of the midst of the fire. 5 Also out of the midst thereof came the likeness of four living creatures. And this was their appearance; they had the likeness of a man. 6 And every one had four faces, and every one had four wings. 7 And their feet were straight feet; and the sole of their feet was like the sole of a calf's foot: and they sparkled like the color of burnished brass. 8 And they had the hands of a man under their wings on their four sides; and they four had their faces and their wings. 9 Their wings were joined one to another; they turned not when they went; they went every one straight forward. 10 As for the likeness of their faces, they four had the face of a man, and the face of a lion, on the right side: and they four had the face of an ox on the left side; they four also had the face of an eagle. 11 Thus were their faces: and their wings were stretched upward; two wings of every one were joined one to another, and two covered their bodies. 12 And they went every one straight forward: whither the spirit was to go, they went; and they turned not when they went. 13 As for the likeness of the living creatures, their appearance was like burning coals of fire, and like the appearance of lamps: it went up and down among the living creatures; and the fire was bright, and out of the fire went forth lightning. 14 And the living creatures ran and returned as the appearance of a flash of lightning. 15 Now as I beheld the living creatures, behold one wheel upon the earth by the living creatures, with his four faces. 16 The appearance of the wheels and their work was like unto the color of a beryl: and they four had one likeness: and their appearance and their work was as it were a wheel in the middle of a wheel. 17 When they went, they went upon their four sides: and they turned not when they went. 18 As for their rings, they were so high that they were dreadful; and their rings were full of eyes round about them four. 19 And when the living creatures went, the wheels went by them: and when the living creatures were lifted up from the earth, the wheels were lifted up. 20 Whithersoever the spirit was to go, they went, thither was their spirit to go; and the wheels were lifted up over against them: for the spirit of the living creature was in the wheels. 21 When those went, these went; and when those stood, these stood; and when those were lifted up from the earth, the wheels were lifted up over against them: for the spirit of the living creature was in the wheels. 22 And the likeness of the firmament upon the heads of the living creature was as the color of the terrible crystal, stretched forth over their heads above. 23 And under the firmament were their wings straight, the one toward the other: every one had two, which covered on this side, and every one had two, which covered on that side, their bodies. 24 And when they went, I heard the noise of their wings, like the noise of great waters, as the voice of the Almighty, the voice of speech, as the noise of an host: when they stood, they let down their wings. 25 And there was a voice from the firmament that was over their heads, when they stood, and had let down their wings. 26 And above the firmament that was over their heads was the likeness of a throne, as the appearance of a sapphire stone: and upon the likeness of the throne was the likeness as the appearance of a man above upon it. 27 And I saw as the color of amber, as the appearance of fire round about within it, from the appearance of his loins even upward, and from the appearance of his loins even downward, I saw as it were the appearance of fire, and it had brightness round about. 28 As the appearance of the bow that is in the cloud in the day of rain, so was the appearance of the brightness round about. This was the appearance of the likeness of the glory of the Lord. And when I saw it, I fell upon my face, and I heard a voice of one that spake." ~Ezekiel 1:4-28

Many philosophers have suggested that this Ezekiel description is a meditation or descriptive of some sort of practice, perhaps about loops of energy, circulation of energy from one chakra to another and intersecting or looping with other energy points outside of ourselves. It is certainly possible that one interpretation of this description could be a metaphorical meditation instruction of circulation of energy. The middle of the wheels can be considered as points, the lightning as lines, the faces can be considered to be as planes, the wheels as further planes, the moving of energy being the focus of the potential instruction, and the vault is a solid or volume.

One of the simplest meditative loops or planes in meditation is to intermingle just a little of both divine masculine and divine feminine energies in the root chakra or guttural area to allow opening of the flows throughout the metaphysical body. Rooted feminine energy intermingles with masculine energy from above.

Carl Jung said many times, in so many words, that meditation is the practice of individuation. It also can be, or most often becomes, a highly individualized practice. You know best where you need opening and increased form and flow. I frequently practiced with loops forming from and freeing up my throat and crown chakras, or circulating energy through my heart, throat and crown chakras as well as other loops at the same time, or wheels within wheels. Be open to practicing individuation as you practice in order to open up your own individualized being and crack through to your true nature.

The complicated and secretive meditation of deep commitment called the Kalachakra meditation has elements of integrating the divine masculine and divine feminine in unity, and more than that, focuses on manifesting world peace.

Kalachakra means time cycle or energy wheel of time. A Kalachakra Mandala is depicted on the cover of The Geometry of Energy. The mandala depicts a plane, but is a picture of a metaphysical temple in the middle of a court. It is an unfoldment of a metaphysical union that can result when the practitioner goes without orgasm, and moreover without ejaculation, transmuting sexual energy into focused thought energy of peace, which is emitted through and to the collective consciousness. This union of individual thought with the wheel of time may lead to orgasmic feelings, and on a divine level is for global peace. One of the main lessons of the Kalachakra meditation is that our inner consciousness cycle reflects, and is tune with the outer consciousness, the universal collective consciousness of the wheel of time. It is a meditation for world peace and for all aspects of oneness to unite.

"As it is outside, so it is within the body." ~From Kala Chakra text

Do you have a certain part of your body that is often injured, and energetically or metaphysically attacked? Then open up your bad arm or knee to a higher form and flow of healing energy. Intermingle energies and use your imagination, which is simply using your mind, to direct and loop the energy through the injury or stagnation, opening up your bad knee to healing energy.

Medicine wheels are meditative circles or planes arranged on the ground using rocks in a circle with a cross or spiraling circle perhaps.

Medicine wheels were used in meditative practices of American Indians as well as Tibetan Buddhists most notably. These mandala shapes form arrangement into healing devices, where distinction between giving and receiving become transparent and all becomes beneficial to all. Performing circle walking or circumambulation around trees or sacred areas connects us with the energy of circulation or planes.

Reflection on transmutation or cycling of energy or idea is a meditation itself. The most powerful transmutation is of a negative into a positive. Doing so depends more on decision rather than situation. When we have a legitimate reaction to a situation, or a near unconscious patterned course, it is our decision. Instead of allowing a trigger to set off a negative downward spiral we can decide to deflect the energy or spiral upward. It is only a matter of decision, being aware of the situation, and then being able to make that decision requires work. Imagine fields or planes in nature, like the rings, or fields of rocks around Saturn, or like the circular air flow of hurricanes and powerful storms as similar to your own power to circulate energy and idea.

"If you wish to understand the universe, think of energy, frequency and vibration." ~Nikola Tesla

The Daoist or tai chi related microcosmic orbit meditation suggests that we form universal attributes as we circulate internal energy between our dantien -a chakra just below the belly button- and our crown chakra. The idea is to generate and circulate energies. Another more high level meditation is known as the macrocosmic orbit. Both of these are overall simple concepts, but allow for near endless and unlimited refinement. In the operation they relay the power of planes, circles, and circular orbits where we connect and integrate energies in a cycle toward refinement.

Circulation of energies is essential for developing vitality of mind and body and it is essential in producing in tangible form or development of intangible concepts. Circulation develops powerful potential and eliminates stagnation.

Clearing Collective Consciousness

The consciousness of individuals can be illustrated as vertical form and flow. Collective consciousness forms and flows horizontally as does interaction between individuals. The planes of collective consciousness and of other individuals intersect with our individual vertical form and flow.

Depending on the level of consciousness of others, and depending on our own level of consciousness, the intersection takes place differently. Sometimes dense planes intersect with us in dense and variously unclear manners, but when we elevate ourselves, the planes of exterior consciousness intersect with our own consciousness in clarity, without obstruction or difficulty. If we are in low functioning state of mind, shifts occur there, if we are functioning at a higher level, higher shifts occur.

Whenever there is activity or an occurrence that numerous individuals observe, because of their own perspective, and because of the condition of their functioning, they note totally different aspects of the occurrence and have a totally different understanding of what happened. The same information may be interpreted totally differently depending on how the event intersects with the individual.

These horizontal planes of consciousness can knock us over, or tip us so that we're unaligned, swaying us to stand on inauthentic, hypocritical, or insecure foundations. When we are rooted and suspended authentically, our own vertical plane of consciousness becomes more and more expansive and more and more retardant to intrusion from the negativity or impact of the inauthentic untruth of others. When we are grounded and at the same time ascended, more of our true nature, the better we are able to comprehend situations, which otherwise may be over our heads or knock us off of our feet.

Situations, circumstances and energy of any sort might be detected and interpreted differently depending on our own level of grounded ascension and untipped verticality. The energy might be understood, or its meaning might be missed overall, or it might even go unnoticed despite still carrying influence. Communication and events are energy loops sent throughout the collective. Sometimes these loops lasso us and steer our thinking and being for some time and often without our awareness. Sometimes we are capable of holding our own no matter what happens.

In order to better hold your own true nature and not be thrown for a loop it is helpful to understand the tai chi principle of Roll Back. It is a movement and idea. The idea is to not allow negativity of others to intersect with your being, but to guide it in a circular or spiraling pattern so that it sweeps by you. The Roll Back idea can be used when such negativity might be occurring to prevent entanglement. Another technique that can be done in meditation after entanglement attempts occur is to imagine extracting the entanglement attempts together and exploding them to be recycled into the earth leaving only your authentic golden self.

    We intersect with energy and reflect energy. We also hold and project energy, and can thereby influence others and our surroundings. Depending on the level of our consciousness and our ability to detect and project we may only detect and project at one level in finite ways. When we start to shine on more than one level it becomes easier to shine on multiple levels, and then infinite levels. This is like the form and flow between two mirrors where suddenly two reflections result in infinite reflections or infinite circular planes of effect. Individuals are capable of transmutation through communication and even simply their thinking and being so that they completely change the dynamics around them.

    In order to change we often wait for the situation to shift to accommodate our intention. In fact, it is best to change our own situation to accommodate the intention. In order to change our state of thinking and being we must change our thinking and being. Meditation practice implements these changes directly and indirectly. A change in posture to a more upright and relaxed position, allowing for proper breath and energy flow, changes our situation. Even if we do not meditate if we simply hold our physical and mental posture in a meditative manner we can implement situation shifts much more easily.

    Build a strong circle of friends and if possible a circle of friends who will meditate with you. When you meditate in a group, energy can circulate in a more substantial manner. When you have a strong circle of friends when you give you also receive, others become an intrinsic part of you and their happiness is your own. This gives new meaning to the idea that what goes around comes around.

When you have a close circle of friends you can expand your notion of who is a friend. The more you see you in people, the more you can expand your sense of belonging to groups of people and people belonging to your group of friends. The more positive you become the more positive people become around you. The feeling of authenticity in yourself brings about realness and authenticity in others.

This authentic feeling is akin to light, in that it eliminates density and darkness and extracts golden light in some unhindered manner as light into dark. The authentic gold within people is extracted by your own golden light. Interestingly the chemical symbol for gold on the chart of the elements is AU, like authentic.

When we meditate in absorption we can loop or cycle energy from point to point, through these points to open and clear. We can do the same with others during meditation making group meditations so powerful. In fact, on a deeper level, as we intermingle in life, we all share energetic loops between us in relationships. When situations come up or ideas are shared there are karmic loops that develop and bond, so use your words wisely so as to build, to be productive and not destructive.

It is important to analyze our relationships with the collective, with others. And it is important to meditate on how mediation of information serves us and how the cyclical flow of our circle of friends is positive and/or negative for our self and others. If their behavior, their thinking and being is negative for yourself and others it's important to cut the loop. Do not let yourself be caught up by the form and flow of negative cycles that may otherwise replay endlessly until you call an end to them in a positive manner acknowledging their benefit and the fact that they're no longer needed.

When the energy loops between you and institutions and/or individuals no longer are of benefit for your individual development, when the loop no longer forms a beneficial receiving and releasing relationship, then the loop must be undone. Often simply forming the words to do so and meditating on it can make the shift or the unlooping.

Everything in nature including your being forms and flows in cycles, in circles. The mandala of the yin yang represents this ebb and flow of nature and time. The cycles become like waves crashing onto the shore. As the waves push onto the shore the prior wave is also receding back into the ocean. Things are constantly in flux, but operate consistently too. Imagine your meditation is a circular cycle, where as we ascend we sometimes descend on our way to higher vibrations and the shoreline. The more we are aware of our consciousness in this way the more we can control and steady our consciousness on its way to the shoreline of understanding.

The veil of mara in the Aum symbol separates the fourth level of consciousness. It is sometimes considered to be an ocean to cross and when we make the journey across we reach true understanding of entirety. There is an ocean to cross and meditation can get us there, but sometimes we falter and stutter because of the storms and currents of the ocean. This is okay. Stay the course. Take advantage of what might be considered distractions or storms and meditate through them to heighten your state of thinking and being.

Imagine everything you require is already inside you. Imagine being all you need yourself as your cycle of energy expands so as to hold you steady amid the turmoil that the collective or mediated consciousness throws at us. Imagine you are all you need to be happy and healthy. Imagine that refining your breath cycle leads to the ability to obtain nutrients and ultimately high quality energy. In fact the more we consciously and meditatively breathe the more high quality energy we have. When you cycle your energy insider you, you end up more stable and more healthy and less thrown off by collective consciousness. When you are in a higher meditative state, mediation is less likely to steer you into thinking you need something outside yourself. Even medication we take when we are unwell often enough simply triggers our body to heal itself, it does not cause the healing, but instigates our self to heal self. Stay true to yourself in your own unique form and flow without allowing mediation to convince you of you, and your needs.

The Solid

The solid is capable of holding volume and incorporates all the aspects of the prior three dimensions of geometry and energy. Points lead to a line, lines lead to a plane, planes result in a solid, a volume capable of holding space. The solid depicts bringing about unity and expansion or rather unity expansion. The solid symbolism is about expanding our sense of our unity with everything.

Buddha became enlightened after meditating under the Bodhi tree for a long time, practicing both circumnavigation of the tree, a walking meditation, and still meditation while seated. After sitting for a long time he became enlightened. He then stopped meditating and had four thoughts to share. They were henceforth known as The Four Thoughts as they were that important.

The first of The Four Thoughts is precious human body, our self as the center point. Impermanence is second, like a line with a beginning and an end. Then karma, the loops between people, places and things, which is like a plane and cycle of energy. Samsara is the last of The Four Thoughts, it signifies the entirety of form and flow on this plane of existence of happiness and suffering.

Without going into detail they represent the idea that we have the precious ability to become enlightened in this lifetime, that everything is impermanent, that everything is made up of and attached to karma or the law of cause and effect, and lastly that we are all a part of the solidity of Samsara, a place of duality.

Karma can be understood as points and lines making shapes. Karma begins as if a bullet triggered by our hand, a consequential bullet that sometimes has instant consequences, and sometimes it's as if it ricochets of off Jupiter before returning. The lines are like the attachments we develop and sustain, that like the term karmic bonds, might restrain us and refrain us and be hindrances to our finding our true nature.

Karma can also be depicted or understood as planes and solids. When we exist in a certain circle of friends we are subject to certain group behaviors, understandings and events, when we live in a certain area we are subject to certain circumstances and situations. Our circle of friends and location are examples of planes of karmic energies. Karma as a solid can be understood in many ways, but in one way karma can be like fire that burns off our potentially hindering cords, the result positive acts.

Karma is the physical manifestation of spiritual energy and karma manifests in four main spiritual formations. There is harming karma or matured karma, knowledge-obscuring karma or stored karma, perception-obscuring karma or present karma, and the last type of karma hinders completely as a combination of the three and is actionable karma.

Karma can be related to the geometry of energy and the four geometrical constructs. The most impactful and all-encompassing form of karma and of energy for that matter is solid, but it is important to note that a solid can become a point, or line, or plane. Spiritual and ethereal intangibles can become physical manifestations and can transmute from one form of energy to another. Each type of energy can be opening or closing, positive or negative.

The fourth geometrical energy is the solid. Solids require a minimum of four points to express. One of the ultimate abilities in tai chi practice and in psychic healing practices is taking the space. The idea is that with focused practice one can gain control of individual and universal chi or energy, or space, and then take and hold space in very tangible senses and in somewhat magical formations as well. This idea is used to return individual strength back to its truth after being taken over by some form of negativity. Influential individuals take the space well.

There are many benefits to meditation just as there are many aspects of reality. One of the most pleasant benefits is happiness. The more one practices meditation the more one practices individuation and empowerment, manifesting in the ability to heal, preserve and change psychologically, spiritually and physically. The ability to develop happiness without and despite the influences of the collective is demonstrable in the exchange of emptiness for voluminous. Depression is the mind promoting emptiness, while the opposite, happiness is the heart promoting voluminous. When we take the space back we can hold happiness like compressed air instead of being depressed by negativity.

Being voluminous includes understanding the void, the space of the solid without weight, the empty intangible interconnectedness of everything. Separation results in depression, connection results in happiness, in unity expansion.

We are trained to exist within depression and in disconnected enclosure. The heart exists within happiness and voluminous expansion. When we take the space we burn up separation and open our energy to entirety.

Imagine a time when you absorbed or created space, or where others did so, or imagine a solid, with a volume of space in nature. Imagine being there and being the unfoldment of the area itself. Allow the space you hold to expand when you are able.

We are taught culturally and scholastically that are minds are in charge. We are also taught that there is only one god. In fact existing in our heart, with our heart in lead is our true nature. In fact there is one god, however one god is depicted and comes in a billion forms. In fact we are all god, for there is only one everything. Despite what you were taught being in our hearts is our true nature and there are many forms of god, many paths to god.

The power of knowing god is infinite, however the power of know the infinite within self is godly. It is knowing god within you, with you and permeating you, and of all the volume around you, that leads to individuation.

There is one mantra in Tibet that stands out among all other mantras. It is the mantra of Tibet. It is Om Mani Padme Hum. This is accompanied by Shri as an activator at the end of the mantra occasionally and somewhat secretively. This mantra is the ultimate mantra in the land of mantras because its primal meaning and ultimate message is to spiritually empower individuals to assist others. It is the mantra, in the land of mantras, because it reflects the very essential point of all meditation and meditative movements- open your heart to be open to the universe, inside and outside, intuition.

The literal translation of Aum Mani Padme Hum is something like universal consciousness jeweled lotus within inner-verse consciousness. One of deeper symbolic meanings, on a spiritual level rather than literal linguistic level, is universal consciousness connects with the individual through the diamond heart, the heart of clarity and all colors. The lotus flower symbolizes such compassionate and dedicated heart space. Aum stands for the macrocosmic universe, mani for the jewel, (reflecting infinitely) padme for the (compassion developed) lotus, and hum for the microcosmic innerverse.

The main lesson and implication of the Aum Mani Padme Hum Mantra, as well as the geometry of energy meditation construct, is that our heart driven consciousness connects the individual with the universal through the point, line, plane and solid process. It's said that therein the mantra is bliss, compassionate course and the power of self-development. Opening our heart space to hold clarity and light leads to being open to the universal energy. When we speak and act from our hearts rather than our guts or our heads we are able to manifest productive constructs rather than destructive blocks.

There are four suits of cards in a traditional deck of cards, but there are also, more esoterically speaking, four suits of tarot cards. And the tarot cards are notably related to the four dimensions of geometry and four dimensions of energy through the four suits. There are swords with points for points, rods or wands for lines, pentacles or coins for shapes, and cups for solids capable of holding volume. The tarot reveals yet another layer to the fourfold dimensions of the geometry of energy.

The cards suggest that it can be useful and beneficial to acknowledge each energy type. And further beneficial to simply be in a state of meditative absorption with one of the energy types that make sense, at that present time. On one level the swords represent focus and stillness of an entirety, the rods or wands represent action and following course, the pentacles represents security and union, while the cups represent holding space and emotions, including love.

Love, compassionate understanding and being, is the most powerful form of energy and itself maybe nearly intangible, but it holds weight and volume for us all, in all types of situations. The best presentation of love directly corresponds to the four dimensions of geometry and is the ultra-important Four Immeasurables of Buddha.

The Four Immeasurables are the four aspects of love itself. The four are the love for self, or the point, the love for others, the linear connection, the love for the happiness of others, the looping giving and receiving, and the love for all things in equanimity, the entirety of all creation equally.

Each stage might be difficult to embody entirely, with love in equanimity for all beings being the most difficult stage to truly bring forth. Understanding living beings through the geometry of energy can assist the process. All life shares equal measure of consciousness, the same life spark. We all have different levels of connection, circulation and potential for unity expansion, but we all are equal sparks. The size or nature of the being does not matter to the equality of the life spark.

These four stages of immeasurable love reflect the immeasurable four dimensions of geometry without any abstraction whatsoever. When The Four are contemplated in absorption great ideas manifest and inner work can be accomplished. Their philosophical value only heightened and their ascetic value only more substantiated in the relation to the four dimensions. The correspondence of the Four Immeasurables of Buddha with what for all extents and purposes are the Four Immeasurables of geometry is mutually validating of their usefulness in meditation and more.

As you practice your meditation you can imagine flowing your form from one dimension to another, conceptualizing one geometric dimension to another, or one idea into another. This idea is illustrated in the highly secretive and esoteric ideas eluding to individuation and finding your true nature, but related to timeless mathematics.

"There are always four ways to look at any three-dimensional structure: as points, lines, areas, and volumes, or as corners, edges, faces, and from the center outward." Michael Schneider, Mathematician

There are many ways to look at self and surroundings. One of the oldest numerological ideas that fused mathematical absolutes with spiritual understanding is the tetraktys or tetrad. The ancient symbol is made up of a ten pointed triangular shape of four rows of 1, 2, 3 and 4 dots. One layer of it represents the mathematical absolute of four ways to perceive space dimensionally speaking. Another layer suggests a meditation in correspondence with the geometry of energy beginning with the minimum point required to represent the single point, the two points for a line, three for a shape and four for a solid.

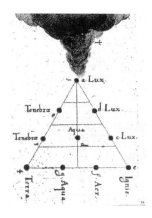

With roots in Egypt mystery schools the symbol was revered by Pythagoras and the Pythagoreans as representative of god and a key to understanding all things. It is related to the four letter word for God, the tetragrammaton and is often used in correlation with the Tree of Life of the Qabalah. In the tetraktys is the counterintuitive reasoning that four equates to ten in the 4+3+2+1 row depiction, and another example of four being representative of completion. Through it was born the Pythagorean cosmology based on four parts; unity, dyad of limit/unlimit, harmony and kosmos.

The tetraktys is said to represent creation similar to many creation annunciations, Yin Yang theory most identically, via one point manifesting two, two manifesting three, and then four and then the myriad things. Another Eastern Esoteric idea that relates to the tetraktys and its four rows of ten points, at least on a subtle level, is what are known as the ten divisions of the universe; the four cardinal points, four midway points, the zenith and the nadir.

Imagine being like a whole volume in nature. Imagine a planet, or imagine being like a cloud, a volume without weight. Imagine being the center storm cloud in the eye of the storm with lightning and raindrops.

And imagine being capable to utilize the storm's power which swirls around you, but you are calm and in the eye of the storm where everything is calm.

We are all like storm clouds. Not the storm itself, but so connected, so revealing of and connected to the entirety that what we do makes or breaks the storm because we are integral. We are composed of and connected to the storm, we are the storm.

Using the four dimensions meditation in a manner that connects us to natural phenomena is wonderful and powerful. Connecting with allows us to connect with our true nature. So wherever you see the four dimensions in nature it can be useful in meditation. Of course practicing as you see fit, with compassionate measures in mind, is the ultimate format in which to meditate.

Taking the Space

In Tai Chi terminology the phrase 'taking the space' is used for martial applications and more importantly energetic interpretations. Its martial reference refers to disabling the structure of the opponent and being intuitively in the right place at the right time. In regards to health orientation the phrase refers to placing wellness where sickness once settled through movement meditation and medicinal herbs. Taking the space concurs with the phraseology and ideology of many psychic, or hands off healing practices too, Reiki, theta healing or Joh Rei. Taking the space is used martially for overcoming opponents and energetically for overcoming opposing energy, and our ultimate opponent, our ego, our inner shadow, in order to regain our true nature. We take the space from our opponents in martial and medical battles. We also take the space during our psychological and spiritual battles. The very word overcome implies the notion of taking the space, come over.

We may have so many cords of attachment that they hold us back from movement, physically and spiritually to the point we rot, as if tied down by many ropes. Whether or not it's the same for everyone, I can't say, but for me when I am around seriously unwell people, in any sense of the word, I see so many vertical cords around them, it's as if they're surrounded by colorful vines, but they are as bars imprisoning them. If we shift or move with intent, if we take the space, we can break the cords. Alternatively when I am around lively natural areas I see points of light, as if each living little being, near as many as the dust, is a point of light, a point of consciousness.

Sometimes it is our experiences that steer us and then have us take the space away from ourselves. If elephants ever run into a negative experience on their migration they will steer great distances to never be close to the place again, just like people. Experiences take the space from us as if we were on our way somewhere and were blocked from that route. Fear is the space taker we all battle, and perhaps the cause of the bars that surround us when we're unwell anyway.

Fear supplies the ego to reinforce the shells which promotes guttural or mental control mechanisms rather than leading from the heart center. When exterior experiences impact us it takes our space and diminishes our power and ability to be in our true nature. Fear takes our space like no other weight or dense barrier can. The void, as Buddhists ponder, is emptiness of fear and negativity, whereas fear is negativity and leads to density and difficulty.

True strength is developed in dedication to practice what's seemingly daunting and fearlessness is developed in learning your infinite potential and your infinite true nature. When you are in your power and true nature you hold space around your physical perimeter and beyond that often enough. When you are in your power you hold space and disallow fear to inhibit and inhabit your space. Whenever someone presents you with a fear summation ignore it, it's a part of their line. No matter how frightful submission to irrational fears is unproductive and restricts our true nature.

The idea of clearing one's space is frequently used as a way to illustrate cleansing, in physical and spiritual form and flow. Sometimes our auras can become cloudy, darkened and grey when in a natural healthy state our auras have clarity with different hues of color emanating from them and preventing lines to bar them in and planes to knock them over.

Just as we use soap to clean our bodies we can use words and thoughts to clean our minds and our spiritual heart-mind if you will. Mantra repetition is one way and one need not know esoteric and ancient mantras in order to benefit for just as some things can be utilized in rituals it is less the thing, but the mind state that imbues power into the word.

Use your thoughts to address your thoughts and feelings which are negative. Remember that negative thinking is most always, at the root, caused by your own negative thinking and that no one can make you feel a certain way, you make you feel the way you do. You are always in control of your feelings and trying to give that power to others is a lie that weakens you.

Fear and negativity can however cause unfolding negativity to bounce around, sometimes boosting itself off of the other negativity it encounters, thereby causing downward spiraling of negativity. Your thinking can clear your thinking and frequently your lacking negative thinking can more clear it also. Think positive and speak from your heart. If you do not understand what speaking from the heart is, use your imagination to begin.

In order to hold space, to manifest a solid with a volume of energy, utilize the minimum number of points to cover entirety. The following rose meditation can be easily utilized to hold space. It takes a minimum of 9 points to create a volume around you. Your center point is one and 4 points in a rectangle above and 4 points in a rectangle or square below create an enclosed space all around you, like so.

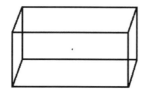

Imagine that the points are roses or any other flower of protection if you have one you empathize with already. Roses are utilized in this idea because of Rosicrucian ideas, I believe. I think this to be the case because the points make an interesting crossing (crucian) of lines. Roses and their essences vibrate at the highest frequency and in this meditation they act like protective and absorbent points. The 9 pointed enclosed volume can be your protected space of varying size, it can be just around you and can expand to hold more space, such as your house or your perimeter when you are out and about.

9 points is the number of points it takes to create and hold a volume of protection with energy lines, when your center is included. When lines extend from these points, the corners into and through the midpoint, you, a rose cross can be envisioned coming through, and extending from you. The cross of these lines and the further enhancement and slight modification of these linear flows soon realizes not just planes but solid shapes. In fact, it creates two pairs of opposing pyramids, instead of tetrahedrons, the simplest of all solids, these are five sided pyramids.

The two pairs of opposing pyramids are the beginning of Merkabas or Merkaba like shapes. Merkabas relate some of the most complex metaphysical and sacred geometrical concepts, all spawning from integration of two of the simplest shapes in opposition. There actually are the beginnings of two Merkabas, or Merkaba like pyramids, one originating vertically and the other horizontally. These pyramids are five sided, including the bases, as opposed to four sided pyramids Merkabas are often depicted as. The Merkaba and Merkaba meditations represent expansive concept of generating and moving energy, where one circulates meditative energies. The meaning of Merkaba has ancient Egyptian etymological roots combining 3 concepts, Mer means counter rotating fields of light, Ka means spirit and Ba means body. In Hebrew Merkaba has come to mean chariot or vehicle. And so Merkaba essentially means counter rotational light field spirit body.

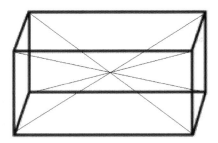

Let your meditation practice become like a rose or blossoming flower. First you are a seed, then you sprout and form a stem taking root and reaching for the sunlight, then slowly you expand with leaves horizontally and finally you blossom like a flower. Be like a rose. Growing, or integrating meditative energy is like growing roses and flowers, even when we have a flowering bush or tree we have to maintain it and care for it properly or it will fall ill. Realize you can only grow meditative energies and plants only so fast and that tending to inner and outer gardens require dedication and continuation despite valleys amid peaks. Roses are the flower of choice for many because their essence vibrates highest of all flower essential oils.

Blessing spaces offers clearing of fear constructs. To bless is to bring bliss. Fear cannot exist when a space is blessed. Blessings may be any number of ritualistic and religious practices or simply having reverence for your surroundings and all the infinite cosmology and biology that enable you to be. Spiritual blessings, the act of saying grace, or speaking gratefully or gracefully takes the space. Graciousness can clear the space, or the volume of the solid with no weight, as can a reverence for all life in the space and all living beings. Imagine all the beings that enable you to live, and all the beings that had been before that progressed your being and be thankful. Grace for all beings is the fundamental notion behind blessing, and will better you and help clear your own space.

All these operations are about release for release leads to realization. Without release of old, impractical delusions, and fears there is no place for new truth and comprehension. Light easily permeates darkness, when the space is open to the light that is when the shells are opened to it.

If we keep things boxed up or psychologically compartmentalized, we maintain separation and disallow light to enter. We do so with our experiences and in our daily life we do so with ourselves. If we compartmentalize our 'stuff' and our existence we ourselves are as if a box of boxes. If we open up to our experiences and ourselves we allow light in and diffuse all the side effects of separating compartmentalized thinking and being.

Fear is a causational cold that can hold people like down like a blanket of snow keeping many inside their ego house. Just like dogs who are aggressive, people who are aggressive often are this way because of experiences that induce being swamped in a fear state. Fear results in preemptive aggression and negativity, often producing the very negativity feared. The opposite goes for positive and compassionate mind states, the positivity often results in positivity. When we realize our true nature we open and expand our sphere of influence rather than shrinking and closing due to fears.

Fear is a solid of nothingness, leading to dense thinking and being, and to living our whole lives afraid to be ourselves, afraid to take a chance and afraid to live with wings spread open to reveal our unique plumage. Most societal constructs insist we think and behave like those around us who are normal under the status quo, so instead of opening up, we close down and retreat to sameness and even resort to nothingness instead of being ourselves, open to everything. We allow fear to infiltrate, and like dogs, react out past dramas and fear plays, instead of being open to the entirety.

Fear leads to separation and feelings of emptiness. Meditation and its potential is as if a box we are afraid to open, but eventually find out there is nothing to fear in it rather only opportunity. Balanced meditation leads to everyness through nothingness, opening up in meditative absorption leads to balanced integration with entirety accompanied by a sense of connection and grace, and the sense of intuition.

"Everything is nothing with a twist." ~Kurt Vonnegut

(Depicted with 0 and zero with twist, 8)   0 8

The meditation the great philosopher Lao Tzu practiced embodied the idea that connecting with nothingness leads to clarity and connection with everyness. Comprehension of spirit leads to comprehension of, and capability to influence, matter.

The Lao Tzu meditation is a physiological, psychological and spiritual body cleanse. One feels into self and notes wherever there is pain or clicks or stiffness or stimulation, or something that is not balanced and not clear. Lao Tzu described these rigidities inside as four strengths. Lao Tzu interpreted strength as related to rigidity and rigidity as related to stiffness and death. Alternatively, weakness is related to softness, vitality and clarity.

"When a man is living he is tender and fragile, when he dies he is hard and stiff. It is the same with everything." ~Lao Tzu

Sit comfortably and upright. Relax your breath, and relax each breath a little more as you connect with the cycle and flow. Allow any tension from the day to sweep away. Imagine the mind and body are condensing and contracting together. Bring your mind, your awareness, down into your belly and wherever you note there is a skip in the clarity, examine it. As you scan your physiological, psychological and spiritual body wherever you note strengths of sadness, anger, oppositional tension, or something that cannot be understood entirely, but is not quite right, feel it out.

In our condensation we can note inconsistencies in clarity and imagine that these are then relaxed away. This process is like turning hard ice into soft water. Imagine contracting the place of strength you come across into a point and allowing it to relax and transform into watery softness.

Feel the points of strength, but it is more important to understand the effects of the strengths rather than causes, and more important to release it than to understand it at all. This process is to release the negativity point into nothingness. The point may release and in doing so expand into a volume of great measure around you and then that space will return to the emptiness pervading, going from point to volume to nothingness. The power of the inconsistent strengths within you and over you is the insignificant. If the strength point does not release move on and bring it with you as you address the next area that is not optimally clear.

"Seek to attain an open mind, the summit of vacuity. Seek composure, the essence of tranquility. All things are in process, rising and returning. Plants come to blossom, but only to return to the root. Returning to the root is like seeking tranquility, it is moving towards its destiny. To move toward destiny is like eternity. To know eternity is enlightenment, and not to recognize eternity brings disorder and evil. Knowing eternity makes one comprehensive." ~Lao Tzu

This Lao Tzu meditation process is like condensing into a point and dissolving into the volume. The condensation and release process in the meditation is very much like what one pictures in absorption. The individual absorbs tension into nothingness and in doing so better connects the microcosm of the individual self, with macrocosm of the universal entirety.

Summation of Masculine and Feminine Energies

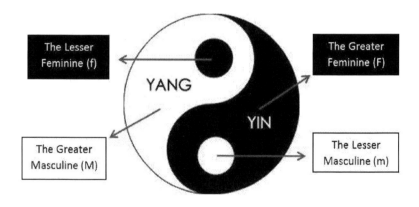

"Gender is in everything; everything has its Masculine and Feminine Principles; Gender manifests on all planes." ~The Kybalion

The four dimensions of geometry applied to measuring objects are highly efficient at aiding comprehension of the physical world. The four dimensions of geometry applied to measuring energies are highly efficient at aiding comprehension of the internal, spiritual and psychological world. Points and lines are masculine, and planes and solids are feminine.

The energy of the divine feminine is both receptive and creative.

The energy of the divine masculine is both reflective and projective.

The potential for these each of these energies to be displayed in one or the other, male or female, is clear, but the tendency of the archetypal energies lean in the above manner. There is creativity in masculinity just as there is reflectivity in femininity. The idea of inner feminine in man and inner masculine in woman is commonly understood as the anima and animus; essentially defined as inner nature containing elements of mutually dependent opposites. The Yin Yang illustrates this with the circles in the swirls.

"The Dao is also the way in the following sense - nothing exists except as a relation with other similarly postulated ideas. Nothing can be known in itself, but only as one of the participants in a series of events." ~A. Crowley

The Dao is made up of feminine and masculine energies, each codependent, mutually arising within the other, and each potentiating the each other. The story of one without the other is fruitless and lacking. The same goes for the story of individuals seeking self-development and divinity as opposed to basic modality. A combination and contrast of energies is essentially required for comprehension and potentiation.

In order to better understand both genders of divinity it is helpful to contrast the feminine and masculine. The divine feminine, which may be as rare a character in the world as the divine masculine, is at least more well understood. The feminine energy is caring in an all-encompassing manner being capable total receptivity to all and adopting all energy. The divine feminine embraces everything in a motherly circle and is capable of creating a whole other being of solidity onto itself, with the obvious masculine potentiation combination of course. The divine feminine demonstrates the caring receptivity inclusion in a circle, and the creativity of generating a whole other being.

The divine masculine embodies reflective and projective energies. Instead of being receptive to energy the divine masculine reflects it. Instead of being creative of volume onto itself the divine masculine is projective of will. The divine masculine reflects energy like a shield or a mirror. And the divine masculine projects energy like a sword or like the singular focus of task at hand.

The divine masculine idea is of a peaceful warrior. This archetype has led to the masculine perversions where warriors are turned into institutionalized soldiers, where the righteousness of self-defense are obscured by war-minded perversions and abusive behavior. The perversions of the mission oriented masculine will is so commonly accepted as normal that women seeking equality among men will do so via military institutions of perverted masculinity. Consider the commonly accepted steering and stupefying in this frequently quoted comparison of love and war 'all is fair in love and war.'

The difference between the divine masculine and the perverse masculine is the difference between a martial artist and a soldier. The most basic principle of martial arts is to **never attack first**. A soldier is paid to follow orders, attack first, or whatever. The difference in divinity and being basic is being helpful and not hindering.

Basic and perverse masculinity clashes -with everything. The reflective energy of mirrors however provides illustration of the potential of the reflective masculine energy. Whatever is shown in the mirror is shined directly back. If the divine masculine is shown quality and caring energy it is reflected in return and if the divine masculine is attacked, with aikido like redirection, the attack is reflected and/redirected. If two or more mirrors are reflecting quality, helpful projected energy than the reflections magnify.

The divine masculine also is projective of energy. The projective energy is a direct willfulness of the individual into the collective. The divine feminine is creative of whole other beings and the divine masculine wills its own being. Of course, the creation of the divine feminine requires at least the energy of the masculine. In the same manner the projection of the divine masculine also requires aspects of the divine feminine, namely the circular inclusion of care and caring.

These energies are theoretic and helpful as a guide for comprehension of self and social situations in contemplation. In reality, in the moment, if there is any doubt as to what embodies divinity, simply seek to enact care. Self-defense and the defense of others requires care whereas bullying and attacking contain no care. The more you push forward compassion and care the more your divinity unfolds.

Further if you are a man contemplate adding receptivity and creativity to your form and flow to engage balance, and from balance refinement is possible. Alternatively if you are a woman contemplate adding reflectivity and projectivity to your own form and flow.

There is an expression in martial arts that embodies the divine masculine or at least presents a notion or rule that is preventative of the perverted masculine. The notion is to **never attack in anger**.

The Geometry of Mandala

A mandala is a visual symbol often utilized in meditation practices and teachings addressing consciousness. The mandala symbol itself is a geometric construction of points, lines, planes and solids symbolizing the universe. Mandalas are geometric designs depictive of the universe specifically inner and outer of course. Other designs are similarly meditation tools, but may not be mandalas specifically.

The visually conceived geometric symbols are visual meditation tools called yantras. Mandalas and all other yantras are visual meditation points of concentration. Yantras are visual meditative tools similar in value to points of concentration. Below is the sri yantra, sri meaning king or most important. Just as we can focus in on one thing with our sight, a yantra is a point of visual concentration.

A mantra is the audio version of a meditation tool. A mantra is an audio meditation tool. Whether the sound of the mantra is a single syllable tone or a series of lengthy metaphysical musings, a mantra is an audio meditation tool. Mantras, as sound vibration, are wavy linear vibrations of connection. A mantra is a wave, a heard line of meditation.

The terms asana and mudra both reference physical positioning. An asana is a body posture as a meditation tool, and a mudra is a hand gesture or hand posture as a meditation tool. Asanas and mudras enable our own bodies to become a geometric representation of a meditation tool and energy. The postures are physical meditation tools transforming self into one's own geometric figure, a plane or field, among the space and sensitive to the space of self and surroundings. An asana or mudra is the meditation tool of physical posturing, and in this way changing our field.

Tantra means unification, or looming/weaving together principles and practices, instruction and individual action. Tantra unites entirety without obfuscation. Tantra signifies confluence and integration; a fusion. It is Sanskrit for loom, the device which weaves together string into cloth. It is an ancient word with many properties and has been variously used to describe the knots of strings weaved together in a rug, and the cord on which sacred mala bead necklaces were strung, (Mala beads are Tibetan prayer necklaces of 108 beads used to assist mentally or vocally repeating a mantra 108 times.) and practices of unification of individual with the universal. Today the word tantra is often used in reference to the union of lovemaking. Though there is also a specific type of yoga called Tantra Yoga, it means unification. Tantra is unseen and imbued and undeniable as the connection between teacher and student or connection among any part of the web of life. Tantra is the meditation tool of volume or unity expansion.

There is the potential of the unification of principle and practice. There is the potentiation of the tantra of yantra, mantra and asana. And there is certainly the lesson of the potentiation of Yin Yang tantra. The combination of Yin and Yang potentials and energies within leads to all sorts of aspects of development. This can be energetically understood in the idea that there are only two types of energies, straight and circular, straight for Yang potentials and circular for Yin potentials. It can be understood on a tangible level that rest and work are both required. When straight and circular energies combine, a spiral is the result. A spiral is one of, if not the highest expressions of energy.

More broadly and generally, tantra notes a mutually accepted connection, a tied knot of intertwined being, like lovemaking, but not necessarily beginning with or limited to the act of lovemaking. Humanity itself is a tantra; a fused weaving knot or many strings, of many instructions and many individuals.

Essentially tantra is spiritual understanding of the relationship and connections between individuation and universal energies. An ancient spiritual philosophy preceding both Buddhism and Hinduism, tantra represents integration, unifying the macrocosm with the microcosm, the universal and the individual, the inner and the outer, the feminine and the masculine, the Yin and the Yang. It also refers to integrative knowledge and its continuation and building refinement through the interaction of teacher and student, signifying union and fusion; the acceptance, integration and transmutation of knowledge between individuals, like the string of life.

Tantric ideas enhance and explore metaphysical merging of ideas and energies. Tantra is the merging of the physical and spiritual, through the merging of the conceptual. In essence, Tantra is the integration of yantra (the philosophy of visual symbols), mantra (communication of audio symbolism) and mudra (our very physical posturing) each of which is important on their own and increasing so when intertwined aspects of yoga, and life. Tantra unites meditation practices and enhances the individual unity expansion with entirety of the universal.

There is not necessarily the need for a specific yantra, or specific mantra, or specific asana in meditation, however each are tools that can be used and considered, and most are most powerful when practiced in unified tantric manner, or tantric mind state. A tantric mind state recognizes unity expansion and aims toward it, rather than cultivating a mind state of separation from integration.

No matter how one approaches meditation the unifying tantra of our meditation principles and practices bring about the unity expansion of yantra, no matter. No matter our level of refinement of posture, we are always in an asana, no matter if we utilize mantra, or yantra, we for the most part still see and hear and those who cannot can still concentrate and connect. And no matter the mantra, yantra or asana, it is the principles behind and pertaining to the symbolism that contains the real power, the highest potential for tantric connection. Yantras, mantras and asanas establish your sacred space and sacred perimeter, but our inner mind state in aimed at uniting with entirety in tantric balance is the most important aspect of meditation.

Seed of Buddha Meditation

One of my favorite meditations directly relates to the four dimensions of geometry, but is extracted from Buddhist lessons. It is one of the most powerful meditations I have learned and as I learned it, Buddha himself practiced and taught this meditation. In fact it's based on The Four Thoughts, which are so important it's said the ideas are the first lesson Buddha taught his followers after attaining enlightenment; hence the name.

I learned this meditation from a Tibetan Buddhist monk from Nepal before I considered the four dimensions of geometry applied to meditation and The Four Thought have little to do with geometry on presentation. On examination however the components of The Four Thoughts and the meditation relate to the four dimensions of geometry directly.

This meditation is direct and simple, but can lead to infinitely complex and profound lessons. The potential depth of each of the ideas in this meditation cannot be understated. And each of the concepts has been elaborated on for centuries since Buddha, and so the presentation here is of course a simplification of the ideas and processes that might be endlessly explored and refined. And that is what meditation is all about really, our own personal inward exploration and refinement.

To begin, sit in a comfortable cross legged position on a meditation pillow. Sit for a time to simply settle into absorption and relaxation, focusing on the breath. The rhythm of the following meditation consists of mindfulness of an idea followed by mindfulness of no idea, where as much as possible we think on nothingness. The nothingness gives us a chance to relax, compared to processing the series of ideas which can all be quite intense. The process can be done in any time period. The point is to cover each idea as deeply as can be, given time or mental state circumstances.

The meditation is formed from important Buddhist concepts. Many meditations are derived from such teachings, Buddhist and otherwise, so that there are lessons in a sense for the secular, and meditation practitioners.

The first part of the meditation consists of concentration on The Four Thoughts; precious human body, impermanence, karma and samsara. This is done by focusing on the ideas through personal experiences and/or universal understandings.

The Four Thoughts not so coincidentally relate to the four dimensions of geometry. The point is symbolizes the individual precious human body, the line symbolizes impermanence, karma illustrates the circular exchange of energy and Samsara relates to the volume.

The precious human body idea essentially comes from the notion that every being is precious for spontaneous Buddhahood could happen at any time, yet humans are particularly well-endowed, for our precious human body is capable of enlightenment in a processed manner. After finding example of how we or others are precious, come to the point of gentle concentration on relaxation. Breathe in a relaxed manner after the contemplation on precious human body then proceed on to the impermanence idea, and then the pause again for gentle concentration on relaxation, and so on, taking however much time is required.

Next is Karma. Most people are familiar with the cause and effect universal law of Karma. However the final thought of the Four Thoughts, Samsara, is less widely known. Samsara is the plane of existence of suffering, of birth and death, we are all in.

The second part of the meditation utilizes concentration on The Four Immeasurables in the same pattern of mindful focus followed by relaxation. There is a modification of the Four Immeasurables order of operation in the meditation, however. They are traditionally presented as; love for self, love for others, love for the happiness of others, and love for all beings in equanimity. In this meditation process begin by focusing on love for all beings in equanimity and end with love for self.

The Four Immeasureables, like the Four Thoughts, are not so abstractly symbolic for and related to the four dimensions of geometry. Love for self is symbolic of individual point, love for others is symbolic for the linear connection, love for the happiness of others is circular and all-connecting and love for all beings in equanimity is voluminous and all-inclusive.

The third part of the meditation is Buddha breath. On every inhale imagine you are removing the ignorance and suffering of others, other people specifically, and those generally locally and globally. And on every exhale imagine you are sending them compassion and happiness.

Imagine you are a conduit of Buddha or supreme consciousness. Imagine that the transmutation of suffering and ignorance into happiness and compassion is all done through you, instigated by you making the connection with above and below.

Imagine lotus flowers from Buddha consciousness being transported through you on every exhale, and on every inhale the fiery pain and suffering of Samsara is drawn into a fiery lotus flower that remains in front of you. This flower burns up the ignorance and suffering drawn into it. Finish the meditation by keeping a lotus flower for yourself, perhaps on the crown of your head, and imagining light shining through you and onto you cleansing you of any leftover negativity.

Each step of the process can take as long as you like or as long as it takes to come to a realization through the first four concepts, send love through the second set of concepts and complete the Buddha Breathing that is inhaling suffering and exhaling healing as a seed of Buddha.

There are of course volumes written on the Four Thoughts and Four Immeasurables and I suggest seeking out more information on them if you decide to delve into this simple and profound meditation, directly passed down from Buddha. These concepts are some of the most simple to illustrate and most profoundly deep to explore.

The fact that each the Four Thoughts and Four Immeasurables each as sets offer stimulating connection to the four dimensions of geometry is remarkable, however the Tibetan Buddhist monk who taught the meditation made no such remark of connection, of course. The Four Thoughts and The Four Immeasureables offer immense practical and meditative rewards, as does understanding the correlative four dimensions of geometry.

Life, in its silliness and suffering offers deep lessons concerning energetics and meditation. The deeper theosophical and philosophical lessons offer multiple applications for observation, of energetics and otherwise, and meditation. These lessons are layered like onions with a wide range of wisdom for life and meditation. The ideas frequently are contained in simple phrases or sets and are intuitively recognized as deeply profound, often without recognition as to why.

The adage of The Wise Monkeys contains vast wisdom and is reflective of the power of symbolism to communicate and instruct on a wide array of understandings from the political to spiritual. I wrote extensively on the philosophical understandings of the Wise Monkeys in The Matrix of Four, The Philosophy of The Duality of Polarity.

Most see the Wise Monkeys as just three; See No Evil, Hear No Evil, and Speak No Evil. There is however the fourth monkey too, being Fear No Evil/Do No Evil. In this adage are political and social lessons, but also spiritual understandings. When the familiar adage and image are applied as potential meditation lessons The Wise Monkeys are linked in a way to the ideas underlying yantra, mantra, asana and tantra.

Calming the physical senses is a great part of being able to use the senses and be sensitive to inward and outward situations. Sensitive observation skills are to be cultivated for living and meditating. In fact hardly a thing can be done without honed sensitivity. The Wise Monkeys have numerous observational lessons, some obvious and some more subtle.

The first monkey is See No Evil, obviously related to yantra. Focus on positivity and beauty and it blossoms. The second monkey is Hear No Evil, obviously relating to mantra. It is an instruction to fill one's auditory senses with again beautiful concepts to bloom such. The third monkey is Speak No Evil. This monkey subtly expresses that should focus on learning, and your practice, perhaps your postures or asanas. When you are not speaking, you can devote time to development, maintenance and healing. Fear No Evil/Do No Evil, the mostly missing fourth monkey symbolizes the stillness and higher being of encompassing tantra.

Tibetan Buddhist healers use a set of observational skills to detect and determine solutions to detrimental health. The Wise Monkeys seem to be related to the format Tibetan healers use for observational diagnosis and prescription without invasive procedures.

Tibetan medicine diagnostics operate on enhanced sensitivity, as well as comprehension of conditions. The first aspect of diagnosis representative See No Evil is simple observation of condition, of dryness or of swelling, or of an imbalanced side step in their gate they may not have been aware. Tibetan medicine also makes simple observation of internal conditions, specifically the tongue and the urine. The second aspect of diagnosis representative of Hear No Evil is taking the pulse. The third aspect of diagnosis representative of Speak no Evil is questioning concerning ailments, of diet, of living conditions and patterns and so on. The fourth aspect representative of Fear No/Do No Evil is the fusion of these elemental observations with the inclusion of intuitive, energetic and astrological observations.

The Tibetan diagnosis procedure is akin to the Wise Monkey archetypes removing the limits placed on themselves so they can make quality observations, though of tangible and basic, toward the complex end of healing. The Wise Monkey archetypes can also be engaged in a more a spiritual manner toward healing or otherwise.

The yantra and See no Evil elements can be compared to inward psychological and physiological observation tools. It also expresses the idea of opening our true seeing ability, as if removing our hands from over our mouth.

The mantra and Hear No Evil elements can be compared to listening inwardly. It also expresses the idea of opening our true hearing ability, as if removing our hands from our ears.

The asana and See No Evil elements enable increased inward sensitivity. We become more sensitive to our physical body positioning and more empowered through healing and strengthening that occurs in recognizing our alignment in stillness and flow. Being more sensitive to our own physical positioning enables higher intuitive sensitivity to that which would have otherwise gone otherwise unnoticed. Understanding ourselves enables us to communicate higher truth, as if removing our hands from over our mouths.

And the tantra and Fear No/Do No Evil elements enable us to heal ourselves, others, and our surroundings, to integrate wisdom and action. It expresses the idea we removed our separation mind state, as if we have removed our hands from our dantien restricting movement and flow of energy.

Adages are powerful because there are the immediate lessons, and even when ignorant of the totality, intrinsic and deeper value or lessons can be somehow sensed. As with The Wise Monkeys there are potential lessons concerning healing and self-development which require some digging to turn up. And then there are all together hidden elements, like the fourth monkey Fear No/Do No Evil being most frequently an altogether missing element. And there are layers like the physical and spiritual observational lessons offered via outward and inward application.

"The stillness in stillness is not the real stillness; only when there is stillness in movement does the universal rhythm manifest." ~Bruce Lee

When we are silent in stillness we can notice the direct link of the universal rhythm, and not only take part in it and utilize it, but unite with it and flow with it. It's as if the universal rhythm is constantly present, singing its song, and when we our quieting our illmindedness and basic conceptualization we can sense it. It's as if the universal rhythm is always singing and whispering to us steadily imploring us to flow and sing along.

How many times have you heard a friend someone tell a story about how the universe was trying to reveal something to them and they refused to see it, or hear it, or be in a state to address it within and outside of themselves. This behavior essentially shushes the universal rhythm, from the universe. In terms of the four dimensions it's like when someone shuts themselves off from the word, shuns others, shields themselves of contemplation of situations, and even shuts themselves in a shell so thick they might not sense the universal rhythm. Of course, inevitably the universal rhythm breaks through, and often enough with a spiritual Two X Four to the proverbial head if continuously ignored. It is helpful to prevent this by looking, listening and posturing oneself in a relaxed manner to observe and absorb the universal rhythm and energies rather than repelling them.

Summation of Vibration

"14 For this cause I bow my knees unto the Father of our Lord Jesus Christ, 15 Of whom the whole family in heaven and earth is named, 16 That he would grant you, according to the riches of his glory, to be strengthened with might by his Spirit in the inner man; 17 That Christ may dwell in your hearts by faith; that ye, being rooted and grounded in love, 18 May be able to comprehend with all saints what is the breadth, and length, and depth, and height; 19 And to know the love of Christ, which passeth knowledge, that ye might be filled with all the fullness of God. 20 Now unto him that is able to do exceeding abundantly above all that we ask or think, according to the power that worketh in us, 21 Unto him be glory in the church by Jesus Christ throughout all ages, world without end. Amen." ~Ephesians 3:14-21

The biblical verse above contains geometrical reference. Measurements of length, depth, width and velocity all work with each other to summarize objects and energies. The theories of special relativity and general relativity, as theorized by Albert Einstein, in part state that reality is four dimensional; made up of length, width, depth and time. Also he states there are four forms of fundamental force in the universe; weak nuclear force, strong nuclear force, electromagnetism and gravity. These all correlate with the Geometry of Energy.

The Geometry of Energy is a four step meditation instruction to meditate and understand meditation The simple form the four dimensions of geometry unfold related to meditation is of concentration, connection, circulation, and unity expansion. The simple Geometry of Energy in meditation enables comprehension of meditation and subtle energy. The correspondence reveals beauty of simplest in the conversion of the mathematical theory into meditative construct. In the simplicity is the ability for you to use as your own tool set, just as math.

The point represents concentration, the line represents connection, the plane represents circulation and the solid represents unity expansion. The point subdues the chattering mind and regains focus. The lines form connection to life forces. The planes enable circulation and integration of life forces. And solids allow the universal to connect with the individual and the individual to connect with the universal.

This extrapolation came to me in meditation as the essence of the meaning of the four dimensions related to meditation. In the chapter layout is the mechanics of the meditation, for each dimension there is the integration and then the disintegration, or a cycle like our breath, the inhale, the pause full, the exhale, the pause empty. When we actualize our own point we disintegrate other's points, when we build our genuine connection we cut cords and attachments that no longer serve us.

Perhaps you can come up with a new concept related to the geometry of energy that works for you better. Perhaps there is another system from the four dimensions or something else altogether that empowers you in your true nature and assists you to better your surroundings in a positive manner. The potential for individuation is part of the beauty of the Geometry of Energy meditation.

First there is a single point within, or self as a point. From out of the point or points there are lines. Lines give rise to planes or loops. And from out of planes or loops are solids of expansive volume. Each is dependent on the other for itself and gives rise to the other. In order to finish meditation it is important to shut down. It is the same as when you drive a car. There are things to do when you arrive and finish driving, you don't just hop out the car. Among the multitudes of meditations there are many different ways to close meditation. For me one of the best ways is to visualize our life giving sun, or your own Sun, as shining bright golden light down on you. Imagining golden light energy clears and closes meditation.

In summation, meditation is what you make it. Even if you don't meditate, according to ancient yoga constructs you don't realize you're are already in a deep meditation and manifesting this reality, for all reality is like a temporarily congealed meditative world, and is born from your meditation. Meditation is universal and is certainly personal. Although there are many formats which work sacredly, there are also many designs which are integrative and when individualized can be as harmoniously powerful as any celebrated theological related practice. You have the innate ability to harness the potential of your true nature through raising your consciousness via mostly invisible inner development. We are all microcosmic reflections of our macrocosmic surroundings and have the ability to integrate, and express universal power to change the form and flows of ourselves and our surroundings.

The Earth has certain energies and certain forms and flows that are obviously different, but part of the same whole. We can change ourselves and change our surroundings with enhanced consciousness and an understanding that the micro operates in the same manner as the macro. As we have points so does the Earth, at intersections of meridians where chakras and vortexes exist, like in Sedona, Arizona, where this idea originally dawned on me. Sedona is one of the most beautiful places on the planet, where desert megaliths of complex beauty reside.

I was there promoting my books while traveling across the country. While there I met one of the most beautiful people on the planet. When we were talking she explained to me her meditation, which was very much like a beautiful interpretation of Ezekiel's wheels, I was for some reason reminded of the four dimensions of geometry. For a moment I pondered them relative to her meditation and meditation in total.

I mentioned the correlation to her and the conversation soon shifted. But I couldn't stop thinking about it. Later that night I was awakened from my sleep as if visited by a stern voice impelling me to write The Geometry of Energy. It was as if someone ordered me to explore the subject and write The Geometry of Energy, or at that point the book with no name.

It all seemed a bit out of the ordinary, but certainly stranger things have happened in Sedona, Arizona. Certainly hearing demanding voices in your dreams is not all that out of the ordinary in Sedona. You might as well expect magical experiences of some sort there.

I began writing it almost immediately as I continued my cross country book tour. I was a point on a line. I was driving a van on a linear highway, on a plane that is the country of the U.S.A., attempting to influence the form and flow of consciousness and effectively the volume of collective consciousness on the planet. I had to write The Geometry of Energy, I felt I was ordered to write it, and I did so mostly in cafes while driving across the U.S.A.

A fantastic shift occurred for me on the road, many in fact, but one in particular can occur for everyone when we unite our individual point with the volume. We are all just a part of the bigger point that is Earth. When I stopped differentiating my surroundings so much and acting to separate everything from me, but instead sought to integrate myself with entirety I became much more open to energy. When I stopped labeling everything and everyone as this or that, and started seeing everything as planet Ethan then I really became open, energy became integrated. You can do the same, this is your planet and all of your surroundings is of and from you, it's planet you. When you do this you raise your vibration and change the vibration around you, expanding your light dimension. Planet you is not a selfish construct, but inclusive and holistic thinking that disables you from the culture of separation. Everything is a reflection of you.

Sedona has a uniquely magical setting in the highly magical region of the Four Corners. Some places are magic in different manners, some places more than others. Everyone and every place have its own unique form and flow, its own unique vibration. Everyone and every place are capable of changing the dynamic of others who interact with them and themselves. Try to interact with the world in positive manner and in positive placement as you proceed as a point on your line, in a region, on the planet.

"Physical objects are not in space, but these objects are spatially extended (as fields). In this way the concept 'empty space' loses its meaning... The field thus becomes an irreducible element of physical description, irreducible in the same sense as the concept of matter (particles) in the theory of Newton. The physical reality of space is represented by a field whose components are continuous functions of four independent variables - the co-ordinates of space and time. Since the theory of general relativity implies the representation of physical reality by a continuous field, the concept of particles or material points cannot play a fundamental part, nor can the concept of motion. The particle can only appear as a limited region in space in which the field strength or the energy density are particularly high." ~Albert Einstein

Sometimes it may be appropriate and helpful to imagine acting as, or considering things in terms of, one of the four dimensions. One can use one's imagination to find the single point or dynamic that can shift a problem into a solution and new direction, or to find the line or route that is optimal for you and your path, or to find a circular cycle that is optimum for self and surroundings, or to find a way to encompass entirety as a sphere capable of holding solidity.

In tai chi practice people say to use your imagination first to feel the chi and then you cannot imagine the chi away. The same goes for meditative energies, sensing intuition and imagining solutions to problems.

One of the ultimate forms and flows, often said to be the very ultimate and pinnacle of all shapes, is the spiral. The spiral encompasses each dimension of geometry. It begins with a point, it is made up of a line, it forms circles and ultimately holds a volume like a solid as theoretically, it continues infinitely. Be like a spiral. Be ready to make accommodation for change in your own form and flow in order to practice individuation and betterment of your surroundings, in order to unify the micro and the macro.

The more you meditate the more individuation you will experience, the more power you will hold and the more capable of resonating your vibration into the collective consciousness you will become. This resonation may feel like a number things including circular resonating vibratory influence, spiral like energy. When your flow and form resonates at a high level it may feel like a spiraling wavy echo emanating from you, beginning in the center and pulsing outward and inward. When you are in a meditative state you can use your power to resonate your being in more capable terms and often enough if it feels right using the spiraling emanating wave. Spiraling energy can go in and out infinitely as expansion.

"You are not a drop in the ocean. You are the entire ocean in a drop."
~Rumi

The four dimensions meditation holds in it the form and flow of the so frequently sought after, manifestation meditation as well. After absorption in a meditative state for a time one can begin manifestation by focusing on the manifestation as a point. Then imagine lines connecting the point of manifestation to you and imagine how the manifestation is in line with universal reality. Thirdly imagine how your manifestation will also manifest or offer something for others in a positive cycling fashion. And lastly imagine that the point of manifestation becomes and solidifies on all levels, capable of holding space of its own. Imagine the point of manifestation becoming a solid and imagine its impact physically, psychically, emotionally and universally.

This manifestation construct can be utilized to bring about heightened awareness, expanded consciousness, and not simply material manifestations. The highest manifestation of course is not material construct, but enlightened higher consciousness.

I find the same format as the manifestation mediation also works for intuitive answer seeking. Whether you seek answers to questions or solutions to problems it begins with a focused question. Whether the question is vocalized or visualized is secondarily important to putting the idea into a focused point.

Focus on the question or the visualization. Then imagine higher energies connecting you with the answer or solution. Then imagine the answer circulating in a way that corresponds with what the higher energy seeks to unfold as well. Then imagine expansion unfolding to the point of completely oneness with the answer so whatever obstructions you might have, whatever blinders on your eyes or plugs in your ears might still be stuck, will soon dissipate. Then imagine recognizing the answer entirely and in entirety. Imagine that it is a step toward your enlightenment, the end goal for practicing intuition.

The idea of Siddhis reflects this form and flow beautifully. A siddhi is a Hindu term referring to magical and intuitive powers. Magic powers are accessible to practitioners, but only the practitioners who know that the ultimate magic is not flight, it is not manifestation of gold, but individuation, developing our true nature and gaining enlightenment, consciousness. It's said there are two types of siddhis those related to magical and intuitive powers and those related to the ultimate magical power, gaining enlightenment and raising consciousness.

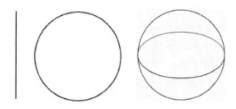

Description of Ascension

All meditation practices assist our ascension to be our true natural self with more potentiation. The cumulative effect of meditation practice, whatever variation, is ascension, and meditation instructions are based on ascension as well. Practically all meditation instruction contains the four dimensions of geometry ascension process.

The point, line, plane, solid progression is mathematical ascension depiction. The energetic related concepts and meditation instruction of concentration, connection, circulation, and unity expansion are essential constructs in practically all meditations, and in the same geometric ascension depiction. With the concepts of the four dimensions of meditation empowering comprehension, the four dimensions become a powerful and simple meditation on its own as well as a way to better comprehend meditation in total.

Concentration: "Be steel wrapped in cotton." ~Tai Chi expression

One's focus should be as such, without tension. Relax concentration on the breath and on your point of light in your heart center. Whether using your heart center, or breath cycle, or a yantra symbol continue to achieve singlepointedness.

Connection: Make connection with contrasting energies of physical and spiritual. Take a moment to secure the connection in concentration of your heart center with the contrasting energies.

Circulation: Move and integrate the contrasting energies of feminine and masculine, of universal and Earthly, and of positive and negative in an electric sense.

Unity Expansion: Enjoy the perimeter awareness expansion of realization of self and surroundings. Observe the observations. Observe the sticky thoughts and emotional patterns as not your own, and conversely observe the arising, revelatory thoughts of the unity expansion as your own. Be in the world as you become in meditation.

Ascension in meditation is like climbing a peak. You are a point and the peak is the point. In order to make connection sometimes several ropes or used and different climbing lines are chosen. Along the way there may be several levels, planes, or plateaus where different aspects of the ascension and the view are revealed. And on reaching the peak there is the enhanced comprehension of self and surroundings.

There are so many narrative accounts and so many fictional stories of ascension that more or less communicate the same truth in the same way. And many of us often have this experience on one level or another at one point or another, where we come to this point in our lives, ourselves.

It essentially feels and goes something like this: After climbing through the jungle, making our way through the grueling forest, dense and bewildering with trails, we came to a clearing on a ridge, on what I sensed must be the very top of the great mountain in the clouds. And as we made our way to the ridgetop and clearing we saw that this was not the top. We saw it was beautiful and magnificent, but it was after all only a plateau. And from the plateau above the bewildering and winding complex of trails ad above the ridge we now stood, we could see in the distance what could only be assumed at this point to be the peak. Perhaps there was a mountain more massive behind it too.

And on the story goes...The reason this story is so often true, metaphorically and specifically, is because that's how it is, aesthetically and energetically. No matter how things go, no matter the plateau or peak you reach, there are always more heights to scale, another plateau or peak above you. As soon as you think you're on top you've stopped evolving, you've stopped ascending. And while you may end up at quite an enjoyable and beautiful place there could be a whole series of heights just beyond you.

The Geometry of Energy is a meditation instruction that you form as your own, through what is conceivably everywhere and infinitely the same and that is mathematical construct of point, line, plane and solid and in meditation it's concentration, connection, circulation and unity expansion. Utilizing the same concentration, connection, circulation, unity expansion concept The Geometry of Energy is also maps the ascension process. The Geometry of Energy also formulates a way toward energy comprehension again utilizing the mathematically sound way of understanding systems, only in this case through meditative examination of points, lines, shapes and solids.

The Geometry of Energy illustrates the ascension process, which is also adequately compared to entering of the tube. It is like climbing a mountain and entering a tube not only because of the rattling dangers one might encounter, but more so because once you begin, there is no turning around. You might stop, but there is no turning around. You must really keep going.

Ascension can be understood through the lightning rod of the Geometry of Energy as a way toward simplification. Through the four dimensions of geometry we are able to engage individuation, understand energy and visualize the big picture as to why this is important.

First you find out what it is you are celebrating as your point. What am I afraid of? Why do I always do X? Then you find your higher point, your more true self. When you know where it is you want to go, when you can visualize the point then you can then visualize your line to it. If the point is something simple like quitting smoking you can then enhance your line, your approach to things accordingly. If the point is something more esoteric or intangible like becoming more intuitive you retain and maintain that point and the lines rise up.

Make connections with lines that more resemble your more true nature, and your becoming, your rising to the next plateau. Become, embody, meditate and chant if you will boldly and simply "I am that...X..." Try to make sure the unfolding of your lines are as unselfish as possible, that is that you do not have to destroy the mountain on your way up it. Put your approaches in modest terms and it great heights can be attained step by step. Often enough if we have a point lines arise.

Thirdly, emancipate your energy to be unrestricted and flow it in a way that opens the linear and circular formations of energy. These openings allow the cocooned you to expand and break out, and fly! I don't care what self-realization or self-actualization you have to practice but circulation must occur and expansion.

Consider the blood being of our physical bodies being illustrative of our energetic bodies. If we are physically unfit our bodies go to shit. If we don't move, or we eat a lot of fat, or if we consume alcohol frequently our blood literally coagulates and slows down. The same is true for our energetic bodies. If we don't practice meditative movement, or meditate, or get involved with nature and our natural state of being the flow of our energetic bodies coagulates too.

Edgar Cayce observed there are four aspects to wellness; relaxation circulation, assimilation and elimination. These four aspects to physical wellness are also applicable to our energetic bodies.

Fourthly is the expansion. Fourthly is the arrival to the peak where the new peak can be sensed. The expansion process is the breakthrough that people talk of and find. It is the crumbling of so many shells that it may seem like a breakdown, but it's a breakthrough. We basically have to find and pry open the cracks, psychologically and spiritually speaking, so that the openings lead to a flooding, but cleansing unity expansion. Or we can just sit there in a half broke cocoon, half way to being a butterfly, hampered instead of freed, like so many figuratively do.

Each energy dimension opens us up more and more to increased ascension because of the enhanced vibrations. Each time you engage this process the more the superfluous aspects of our character fall off. The more we move energy the more the unnecessary add-ons of our induced masquerades, the less-real pieces of our psychological makeup, the constructs and shells that otherwise restrict our true butterfly nature, all crumble from the cocoon.

Breakthroughs are often painful at one stage or another, and certainly during the unity expansion process things tend to break. The more one takes part in your own ascension process the more likely things will break on your way to becoming, until the shell of your ego must be broken too and then slightly modified, maybe with restrictions, returned to working order. And almost certainly, no matter how far you go there is almost always further to go. No matter how your level of being changes there is practically always another higher summit to surmount. Concentrate, connect, circulate, expand unity.

Ultimately meditation is about blending your singlepointedness with the entirety of all, to expand your connection as one singlepointedness with entirety. Meditation enhances our enlightenment and our control of ourselves. Meditation is a way to foster our best, not our best meditation, but our best meditative action in the world. The point of meditation is to enhance concentration to make better your ability to form connection, circulation and unity expansion among energy, including tangible basic interaction.

The point of meditation is to gain enlightenment in the long term, but also to gain enhanced ability and increased sense of peace in the short term. Meditation assists our manifestations inwardly and outwardly. Despite the innumerable variations of things we do in life, how we create and manifest onto the world is essentially the same. Though the idea of manifesting or creating can be esoteric, it is actually totally straightforward and simple and related to the four dimensions of geometry.

The first stage of the manifestation of idea is a thought. Thoughts are encapsulations of ideas. Thoughts are like points. The next stage to bring a thought into reality is to form emotional connection with it, to embody and emotionally conceive the thought. Emotions form linear connections. Emotions are like thoughts that have coalesced connection. The next step is to verbalize and speak on it. Our speech, even a single word, forms a plane where encapsulated points of ideas link together. A picture paints a thousand words and a word paints a thousand pictures. And lastly is the solidification of action itself. We are capable of thinking, feeling, speaking and acting. And our thoughts are like points, our feelings like lines, our words like planes, and our actions like solids.

Meditation is transformative. It assists us in our individuation and enlightenment process and directly contributes to our ability to create, from the mundane to the fantastic. Our creativity flows in a manner in accordance to the four dimensions; the focused thought is coalesced and connected into an emotion and then the spoken word is a plane of connecting points of formation before ultimate becoming the solidification of action.

In this sense the word is a sort of magical instigation and from where transformation into solidification begins. Undeniably we have all had someone say something to us that influences us, our direction. Words have a bright power and energetically speaking words are like a flash of influential formation with thought and emotional power as their source.

Words are transformative for words have the power to bring the intangible into being. Energetically speaking, words and statements look like a flash of a circular plane on which are points of insight with numerous connections to other points of insight. Meditation becomes our best tool to assist our becoming and assist our being. In the most direct manner meditation constantly upgrades our thoughts, our feelings, our speech, and our actions potentially continuously.

"The key to growth is the introduction of higher dimensions of consciousness into our awareness." I couldn't find source for this, but appreciate it so. It's attributed to Lao Tzu.

Unity Consciousness

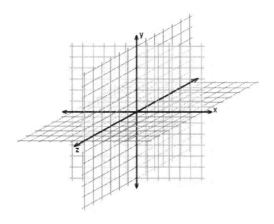

Most often when the term 'four dimensions of geometry' is mentioned, people generally assume the subject is about the mapping of a place in coordinates. A coordinate in three-dimensional space is a point of intersection of three lines by way of three directions, or three dimensions. One line goes up and down, another goes forward and backward, and the third goes across, left and right. The lines can also be imagined as planes intersecting in the same manner.

The first three dimensions are spatial, and the fourth dimension is temporal, the fourth dimension is time. Time, including the past, present and future, is the fourth dimension. With these four dimensions we can precisely point to location in time and space.

Each of the four dimensions are based on contrasts or polarities. There is up /down, left/right, and forward/backward in the spatial dimensions, and there is also fundamental polarity in the alignment of the lines or planes of the dimensions.

The temporal dimension is not just the contrast of past and future. Quantum physics and metaphysics alike suggests there is time and timelessness. The temporal dimension of time is past, present and future contrasted with timelessness. On one end of the contrast of time is it being everywhere and yet in nothing, the other end of the contrast places time nowhere and yet in everything. Conceptualizing timelessness within physical orientation is difficult for it is metaphysical. Comprehension of timelessness is related to quantum physics for we supersede the limitations of basic cause and effect of space time. Consciousness rules space as well as time instead of space and time confining and determining all.

Tibetan Buddhist concepts specifically refer to four aspects of time; past, present, future, and timelessness. The fourth dimension of time (past, present and future) is timelessness. One way to begin to imagine the concept of timelessness is through consideration of the Chakra system. The Chakras are sometimes associated with organs and glands, and are said to spin clockwise and be stacked in a certain layering, but Chakras are not fixed in time, nor space. The Chakra system exists in a way that is beyond three dimensional placement and time restriction in an amorphous condition in the space of timelessness. When biological position is used to relate ideas in the Chakra system it pertains to symbolic aspects of the Chakras.

"Time is the following; that being which in as much as it is, is not, and in as much as it is not, is. It is intuited becoming." ~Wilhelm Hegel
*Questionable accuracy of the source of quote, however the idea itself is splendid enough to be worth mention.

Consciousness measured in quantum physics experiments bypasses the typical limitations of space and time we have become accustomed to, and perhaps also accustomed ourselves to. Meditation enables better understanding of timelessness and potentiates our quantum consciousness. Meditation enhances the potential we might not be constricted and hinged by sociological and psychological limitations we have set upon ourselves as well as constraints upon our very own consciousness set up by our own consciousness. Meditation results in being more in tune with space and time as well as feeling somehow beyond space and time. Meditation is like quantum physics as both deal with energy unrestricted by the constrictions of space and time.

Without the hindrances of our very own thoughts and emotions, and our very own physical limitations, our minds can move beyond space time limitations we have set upon ourselves in a quantum consciousness manner. When we are operating in quantum consciousness strange things occur. Placebo healing that is theoretically impossible transpires as does other correlating and coincidental events that defy the typical four dimensional physical constructs and limitations. Comprehension of timelessness opens up quantum consciousness, and meditation provides for the clarity needed for comprehension.

Another set of four in geometry often conflated with the four dimensions of geometry is the four measurements of height, length, width and breadth. The importance of the four dimensions of geometry; points lines, planes, solids, is perhaps mixed up with the importance of these other sets of four within geometry so much that each might have their significance diluted. Each of these sets of four are important on their own as it concerns measurement, and powerful as tools to contemplate intangible energy as well.

The ability for concepts to be used outside of their original design is revealing of their power as a comprehension tool. The more potent tools are compatible and applicable to many systems. Metaphysics is based on the integrative operative rather than compartmentalization. Such tools go beyond their original design, so as to become metaphysical. Quantum consciousness and the meditative mind state operate in this same manner, going beyond the obvious dimension of placement. Quantum physics suggests there are perhaps connections through the temporal structure that supersede the spatial, and further aspects of consciousness that supersede the temporal structure as well the temporal. A major part of quantum physics contains the uncanny idea that what we commonly understand as being insubstantial and intangible is actually more substantial than what we perceive as substantial and tangible.

Quantum physics experiments suggest that consciousness can influence the trajectory and nature of light in manners that are not confined by time and space. The idea that consciousness can influence anything at all, let alone light, let alone light in a manner that supersedes time is astounding. That consciousness influences light in this manner is astounding on its own, and in the implications and questions it raises, but sensible perhaps that this influence is not restricted by time and space considering the potential exists at all. What is again remarkable and strange is that consciousness influences without trying to do so, by simply observation.

The quantum physics of our consciousness demands an enhanced understanding of the spatial and temporal dimensions. Moreover, this dynamic or power apparent in quantum physics experiments demands and enhanced understanding of our very own consciousness and suggests the value of meditation to employ refined conscious observation.

This dynamic, this consciousness potential may have been known as a Siddhi at among yogis. A Siddhi could be understood as quantum consciousness cultivated through meditation. Gaining siddhis is not the point of meditation, and further it is said that if gaining Siddhis is your focus in meditation then they will not become. Siddhis are side effects of meditation practice toward gaining enlightenment such as intuitive awareness enhancement.

Meditation practice of whatever sort assists gaining clarity. The more clear we are the more easily we realize everything is connected in manner more substantial than material, in a way resembling unity expansion totality. The less muddied our perception the more we are able to visualize, perceive and act unhindered. The more clear we become the more we recognize and unite with the light.

The more basic our level of comprehension, the grosser our perception of totality, the more things we miss altogether. The more basic and stuck our perception the more basic our realizations. The more refined our comprehension, the more sensitive our perception the more easily we note that the origins of entirety is light and energy. The more we raise our spirit the more capable we become of moving past spatial and temporal limitations in a timeless manner, exemplified in eliminating negative patterns and enhancing intuition, for instance.

The more refined our senses and sensibility the more real and substantial the immaterial becomes and the less important the material becomes. This idea is at the core of the Four Worlds of The Kaballah, and the corresponding ten Sephirots (meaning counting) of the Tree of Life. The Four Worlds of the Kaballah are sometimes known as Emanation, Formation, Creation, and Fabrication. We exist in the world of fabrication, the material. The Four Worlds and the ten attributes of The Sephirots contain numerous lessons of great depth, and at the basis or core of The Tree of Life of Kabbalah is The Four Worlds. One way to break down the etymology of Kaballah is by noting two major words, kabb or kaba is Hebrew for cube, and alah or Allah is God.

The world of Emanation is the spiritual void and from it the other worlds originate. Creation originates from the most subtle world of Emanation, Formation comes from Creation, and the material world of Fabrication comes from Creation. Our world of material existence, the world of Fabrication, begins in the spiritual world of Emanation and the energy moves through the other worlds before manifesting here.

~The world of Emanation correlates with the element of fire, the Tarot symbol of wands, the dimension of the line, and our will. The linear wands symbol is masculine. When viewed internally this world correlates with our mind in total, a mind of higher thinking and being, a unified brain connected to an open heart.

~The world of Creation correlates with the element of water, the Tarot symbol of cups, the dimension of the volume, and our emotion. The cup is feminine. When viewed internally this world correlates with the Neocortex, the contemplating brain.

~The world of Formation correlates with the element of air, the Tarot symbol of swords, the dimension of the point, and our thought. The sword is masculine. When viewed internally this world correlates with the Limbic System of mammalian brain, a slightly higher thinking than the Reptilian Brain.

~The physical world of Fabrication correlates with the element of Earth, the Tarot symbol of coins, the dimension of the plane, and the material. The coin is feminine. When viewed internally this world correlates with what is known as the Reptilian Brain.

Each dimension contains masculine and feminine potentials, but each tends to embody one or the other more so.

Our physical senses only note a portion of the known physical world. What we do not notice, we frequently assume to be nonexistent even though there is much more going on than we are able sense. It is only natural to initially assume there is nothing more, it is juvenile to maintain this perception though. According to the Four Worlds concept of The Kaballah it is the spiritual world of Emanation that is more substantial and more real and from which all begins. It is there that subtle energy originates, and from which all else is dependent on. And most people are mostly restricted from sensing this due to the limitations of our material being. When these limitations are unconceived, the corresponding lacking clarity is only increased.

Only through gaining clarity do we develop sensitivity to the roots of reality. The situations of the material realm of Fabrication originate in the spiritual realm of Emanation. The material reality begins as spiritual energy and traverses through the other worlds before being noted by our physical senses. So despite our basic notions of material and immaterial The Four Worlds puts forth the idea that what we perceive as the immaterial is more substantial, more primal, and more significant than what we perceive as material. The world of Emanation corresponds to the world of timelessness, the void, the divine light.

The Four Worlds of The Kaballah and ten attributes of The Tree of Life reflect and are related to the Tarot cards of four suits, each with ten numbered cards. The relations may be simply in their shared metaphysics, but it's likely more tethered. Metaphysics seeks to find the connections beyond space time and the humanity beyond culture or nation. And so it is really no wonder that metaphysics in relation to such subtle energy is as intricately related as The Kaballah and Tarot seem to be.

"Learn how to see. Realize that everything connects to everything else."
~Leonardo Da Vinci

The Tarot cards are mostly known for their use as a tool to intuit information through the cards and consciousness. Card readings pierce space time so to speak, to view timelessness and thereby make predictions or readings based on the energy of the cards. Yet the Tarot and Kaballah are mainly about measuring energy and communicating/interpreting the energies and life lessons. The depth of the Tarot and the Kaballah is potentially limitless, and yet there are profound primal lessons which maintain their profundity and applicability no matter how many other concepts one learns.

The Tarot is made up of 78 cards. The Major Arcana of 22 cards, numbered 0 through 21, and the Minor Arcana which are the four types or suits. There are 14 cards each of the swords, wands, pentacles and cups of the Minor Arcana, 56 in total.

The Tarot cards are said to access the divine feminine energy, the Universal Yin energy, the timeless Akashic, so as to contemplate, intuit, and comprehend the spiritual and more subtle worlds so as to more accurately the material world. When the spiritual worlds are understood the material world becomes elementary to the point of predictability. The divine feminine energy of Tibetan Buddhism is specifically the Goddess Tara. Tara is most known for her form as Green Tara however there are 21 colors of Tara, akin to the 21 numbered cards of The Major Arcana. Tara is said to offer healing and liberation in manners that pierce space and time limitations when her mantra is repeated with devotion and repetition. In Vedic concepts 21 symbolizes the human form, 20 for each digit, our fingers and toes, and 1 for self.

The Unification of these metaphysical traditions, each capable of standing on its own is each enhanced by the correspondences, numerically and energetically. The metaphysical unity of the diverse traditions harkens to their value for individuation, intuition and energy comprehension, but also points to the true unity of humanity. The sacred geometry of energy and energetic relationships within the metaphysical concepts of Kabballah, Tarot and Tara clarifies and unifies, along with offering signification of each concept. Connecting such traditions, which had possibly been prior split in a fashion similar to the division of (metaphysical conceptualization concerning subtle energy) language in the allegory of The Tower of Babylon, leads to enhancement of the ideas.

"When all activity has ceased and you simply are, just to be, that's what meditation is. You cannot do it, you cannot practice it, you have only to understand it. And whenever you can find time to just be, and drop all doing –thinking is also doing, concentration is also doing, contemplation is also doing– even for a single moment if you are not doing anything and you are just at your center, utterly relaxed, that is meditation. And once you have got the knack of it you can remain in that state as long as you want." ~Osho

All too frequently we are caught up in mental, physical and emotional turbulence resulting in lacking clarity and even rigidity. Lacking clarity we cannot get the knack of being so to speak because we are stuck in the basic and the grossness rather than void of such. Rigidity in thinking and being processes result from lack of clarity and negative patterns emerge. When we approach the energy of systems rather than the results of the energies we can naturally better understand, overcome and influence. In order to gain clarity in a body of water settling must occur, a settling of agitation. In order to gain clarity in our own body a settling must occur, a settling of attention. Stillness, rather than insistence, offers opportunity for settling of attention, and clarity.

Many times we might have an idea of what we are looking to accomplish or develop in our meditation practice, sometimes we can use meditation as opportunity to simply get out of our own way, to move beyond our limitations and our pains. Without clearing the mud of the mundane physical, mental and emotional attachments and so on, we will not be able to instill the feelings of oneness with the universal, the unity expansion. We have to feel in order to reveal and then heal using our attention, or without our attention we settle for discord and muddied perspective, and even forget that we are lacking clarity.

Body Scan Meditations

There are many particular meditation practices, being there are many ways to reach peace and clarity, and many reasons to otherwise meditate. Meditation comes in many variations because there many originations, many starting points, and many different phases of our journey.

As Osho so sweetly summarizes, if we can reach some clarity, we can find more of it for longer periods. And this can lead to all sorts of profundity. No meditation practice exists solely for itself, meditation is a tool to reach the destination of clarity, of unity expansion. The processes of mindful meditations, including body scans, are no different. The processes are utilized to enhance clarity which is beneficial in innumerable ways including initiating healing.

Because clarity is so essential to experience the meditative mind state, and because clearing imbalance and blockages is obviously essential to resonate with entirety towards unity expansion many different systems elaborate on clearing and healing. The following two similar body scan meditations are healing practices from Daoist and Buddhist traditions.

From my experience with Daoist and Tibetan Buddhist meditations specifically, as well as less rooted ideas, there is a systematic approach to this clearing. The ability to have a moment of clarity, of just being, can require a process, a trip. Clarity is likely not achieved by forcing away thoughts, but rather by a thought process.

Meditation in total, and body scans in particular, assist us in moving beyond embodied limitations and attachments, and in initiating healing. Meditation helps us to experience insubstantial and intangible energy as being more substantial than what we mostly perceive as substantial and tangible. Feeling subtle energy increases sensitivity to stagnation and enables the power of our attention to move the energy stagnation, or inflammation.

One of the main commonalities of the body scan processes for clarity is the flow of energy downward beginning from the crown. When we imagine energy flowing from the crown of our head downward and out of the feet we release tension and stagnation. Alternatively if we practice a flow upward from the feet to the head we obtain energy. I realized this through the process of practicing Tai Chi meditative movement, in which we warm up and cool down.

When we begin with our crowns and proceed downwards we release energy, when we begin with our feet and proceed upwards we obtain energy. Don't bother the mind with thinking about releasing specifically, as it happens on its own due to the flow of the process itself.

The main difference between the Daoist and the Tibetan Buddhist flow of the body scan process is that the Daoist process clears energy at specific physical locations such as the muscles, bones, organs, nerves and even cells. The Tibetan Buddhist process focuses on clearing the chakra systems or chakra layers through the regions of the body. The flow of the process is of a clearing light moving through the system. The light is sparked in our imagination and attention. Our imagination is the best way to engage with the spiritual world, or the world of Emanation, of creativity. Imagine the clearing light moves stagnancy and inflammation on physical, emotional and energetic levels.

Sacred geometry concepts, meditation practice, quantum physics, and even the Kabballah and The Tarot all utilize and empower the idea that our consciousness supersedes space time limitations. These metaphysical ideas embody and exemplify the idea that the ocean is in the drop as well as the drop being in the ocean.

The spiritual realm of nothingness and timelessness is not limited by the constraints and conditions of space and time. Sacred geometry concepts and meditation practices enable us to surpass the imposed limitations of space time as revealed through quantum physics experiments and as we've all likely experienced through revelatory dreams. As one conceptualizes the energetics of the body scan meditation process keep in mind that the potential of the infinite universe is also within the finite individual, that the cosmic is in the atomic.

Imagine that the life giving energy of The Sun, or your sun, clears and enlightens the areas as you move the energy via attention and imagination. Astrological influences, the Hermetic Principle of the micro reflecting the macro or as above so below, as well as the feeling of unity expansion all point to the power of unity of individual connection with the universal. Meditation enables removal of the barriers towards unity.

We can see and sense some of the influence of the celestial bodies, The Moon's influence on the on the oceanic tides for instance. This visible result of physical positioning changing situations is detectable with the basic senses and orientation, the more subtle influences on situations require more subtle senses and orientation. So just because astrology seems like energy that can be easily ruled out it is actually energy which is more accurately simply highly difficult to determine. Such subtle energy is imagined as we clear our bodies with our point of light.

Both the Daoist and Tibetan Buddhist traditions begin with simply breathing for a time to steady the system before beginning the process. These meditations operate on being thoughtful, but relaxed. In being thoughtful of the process we become less susceptible to be called like a monkey to swinging on vines of circling thoughts, thoughts that go back and forth, and do not have a process of progress. Meditation processes keep the mind steadily directed toward the meditative state. And thereabouts, as well as on the way, are opportunities for moments of just being.

The Daoist healing process is normally done lying down as flat as possible on your back. Settle and relax and then begin to bring your attention to the golden starlight at the top of your head concentrated into a single point. The more one knows about biology the more one can apply the specifics of moving the light through the various parts of the body, stopping to enlighten the glands, organs, sinews, muscles, bones, nerves and cells, and especially wherever there might be a stagnation of chi so to speak, an injury or inflammation of some sort. The process can also be as simple as imagining the warming, healing light, the inner smile, moving along through the areas of the body beginning with the crown of the head and unfolding opening simply in a downward and clearing manner. Imagining the simplest biological parts; head, neck, shoulders chest, heart, stomach, waist, etcetera is wonderful and anyone is capable of doing so. Refinement of the attention of the inner contemplation from there is simply like applying more mindfulness into the process. The more specific one's attention is to the minute parts of the body the more clearing can potentially take place.

After imagining enlightened awareness through the entirety of your body bring the point of light to your center, your dantien. Imagine the point of light enlightens your entire body. Settle into the feeling of being and flowing in unity with entirety to close.

The Tibetan Buddhist practice is normally done sitting in a comfortable cross legged position, perhaps sitting on a pillow, though any meditative posture can be utilized if sitting is a strain. Settle and begin the process by imagining a lotus flower above one's head and then a pure clear tigle of light above it, a single point of energy, that spark of life, a speck of The Sun, or your sun. The tigle enlightens the five main chakra wheels or layers in this process; The Crown, Throat, Heart, Sacrum and Root Chakras.

You can perform this meditation for as much time as one is comfortable, and be as contemplative for as deeply as one is comfortable. The essential aspect is to forgive and let go and in doing open up to clear more blockages with the light so there is again harmony and smoothness. A basic result of the opposite mind state offered in this analytical healing meditation, is someone who takes issue with, and purposefully does not think about a certain subject. Thereby there is great issue with it whenever it does come up because of blockages and stagnation.

The main process unfolds in this fivefold manner. First we bring light to our head region and we forgive and thereby clear the thoughts we had which were not compassionate in order to clear stagnation around the crown chakra. You can spend as much time considering each chakra as is comfortable.

Secondly, we bring light to our throat region and we forgive the words we spoke and clear the words which were not compassionate to clear the Throat chakra. Problems with the physical area of the throat are generally associated with the throat chakra. If one has inflammation, or injury, in an area near a certain chakra spend a moment or two longer there.

Thirdly we bring light to the heart and chest region and clear the emotions we felt which were not compassionate to clear the heart chakra.

Next we bring light the lower gut and clear the actions we took which were not compassionate to clear the sacral chakra.

Lastly, we bring light to the bottom of the spine and clear the energy which is not compassionate and the karma of the root chakra. Clearing this energy we bring attention to attachments from outside of ourselves, this can mean our families and ancestors, and those in our area presently, and who came before us and built what is now the status quo, or any energy being outside oneself that you conceive.

To close this meditation process a healing mantra might be utilized, or your one personal affirmation in mantra, perhaps spoken only internally. Finally the entirety of the chakra energies conceptualized and perhaps differentiated come together in one concentrated spark of light representing our core self. Our concentrated individual point of light then dissolves and becomes one with the flow of the entirety of the universe and thereby a seamless integration of entirety, a unity expansion. In this closing aspect of the practice there is the obvious use of the point of concentration followed by the unification of individual with the universal portraying unity expansion of volume.

Both of these healing meditations can be called versions of a body scan meditation, and are perhaps more specifically are the origins of the idea. These practices involve imagining enlightenment. That is to say, we imagine light coming in from head shining and moving down to our toes clearing us of blockages and obstructions to wellness and enlightenment. Being mindful of ourselves while practicing meditative movement or when in still meditation enhances mindfulness as well as the benefits of meditation. We note the stagnation and move through it or otherwise address it to create flow.

"Geometry, coeternal with God and shining in the divine mind, gave God the pattern... by which he laid out the world so that it might be best and most beautiful and finally most like the Creator." ~Johannes Kepler

Some meditation processes might seem complicated initially, but like any practice that at first seems abstract and complicated, it soon becomes sensible and simple. Meditation can potentially endlessly refined and more thoughtful. It is not the point to strain to complexity, but rather to offer a path of thought so that the mind does not wonder off into some negative construct.

Wherever there is a meditation practice with initially perplexing concepts remember the idea behind the initial complexity is to offer a positive path of thinking which prevents being caught up in mundane or negative cycles of thinking. A path of process actually quiets the chatter, whereas no process provides for the chatter. Processes offer pathway to more moments of simply being. Thoughtful processes enable clarity, especially when attention to clarity is part of the process itself, so that moments of simply being, totally unfettered, are attained, prolonged, and maintained.

Ethan Indigo Smith authored The Geometry of Energy after penning *The Matrix of Four*.

Ethan can be found on the usual social media platforms.

Please leave a review on amazon.com for *The Geometry of Energy*. Reviews and recommendations make all the difference for an independent author. Thank you.

The Geometry of Energy inspired the simpler and more nondenominational *Geometry and Meditation for The Youth* for home and school.

Ethan also wrote *108 Steps to Be In The Zone, The Tao of Thoth, The Little Green Book of Revolution, The Tai Chi Pill* and *The Complete Patriot's Guide to Oligarchical Collectivism*.

Made in the USA
Columbia, SC
22 June 2021